The 7 Pillars of Wealth

A PROVEN SYSTEM FOR BUILDING WEALTH ACROSS MONEY, TIME, AND ENERGY

XUFENG (BILL) HUA

SEVEN PILLARS SERIES

Artificial intelligence tools were used during this book's research and structural outlining. All final editorial judgments, fact verification, and citation review were conducted by the author and a human editor.

First Edition: April 2026

Published by Buwa Inc.

Library of Congress Control Number: 2026908412

ISBN 978-1-972908-00-6 (eBook)

ISBN 978-1-972908-02-0 (Paperback)

ISBN 978-1-972908-01-3 (Hardcover)

Seven Pillars of Wealth is part of the Seven Pillars Series.

Important Note

This book is intended for educational purposes only. It reflects personal frameworks and perspectives on money, time, and decision making.

It is not financial, investment, tax, or legal advice. Every situation is different, and you should consult qualified professionals before making financial decisions.

Think of this book as a set of principles to consider, not as instructions to follow.

Contents

Introduction

Money doesn't shout; it presses quietly

"The biggest mistake investors make is focusing on returns instead of focusing on risk."

— Howard Marks, *The Most Important Thing* [1]

Howard Marks was talking about investing in the above quote, but the same mistake can appear long before anyone ever buys a stock. It shows up quietly in everyday life.

A knock at the door. A phone call that was never made. A couple having a conversation late at night, when their children were supposed to be asleep. None of these feels like a financial decision, but each of them is. People are not reckless or irresponsible. Still, something feels heavy in these moments. That weight is fragility.

I have seen capable, disciplined people live with constant financial pressure, not because they lacked ambition, but because they were building progress without structure.

They focused on growing income but not protecting it. They made good decisions, but those decisions were not well connected to each other.

That imbalance created a specific kind of stress—not panic, not chaos, but something quieter and more exhausting: the sense that one mistake could undo everything.

Money felt heavy long before I understood why. I grew up in a family where money was uncertain. Years later, working in investing, I saw the same pressure at every income level. I now work as a hedge fund CFO, where I've seen these patterns play out repeatedly across individuals, families, and institutions. Different numbers, same underlying pressure. That's when I realized the problem wasn't income. It was structure. That insight became the foundation for everything in this book.

My family worked relentlessly and still never felt secure. Our small businesses would first show promise, but then fade. When opportunities disappeared, my parents left to find work elsewhere. Responsibility arrived early in my life. Clarity came much later.

In that environment, I formed a belief: if life was going to change, it would start with me. That belief pushed me toward education and opportunity. It also came with debt, which my family carried so I could have those chances. I felt that weight every day.

As my career advanced, the outside story looked clean. Inside, things still felt fragile. Every incoming dollar had a job to do. Every decision carried pressure. I repaid my debt, supported my family, and spent carefully; but even as my income rose, I still felt a sense of urgency.

For years, I focused almost entirely on money. Earn more. Save later. Fix everything after the next milestone. Then, slowly, something shifted.

I began saving and investing consistently. The amounts were modest, and the progress didn't feel remarkable, but it was steady. My anxiety softened. Decisions became easier. The sense of pressure began to lift.

I was not wealthy, but I was no longer fragile.

That was when I understood what most financial advice misses. Wealth is not built on money alone. It is built across three resources: money, time, and energy. *Money* is measurable. It is tracked and optimized. *Time* is limited. Once spent, it cannot be recovered. *Energy* is your capacity to focus, decide, and act consistently.

THE WEALTH TRIANGLE

—— HOW MONEY, TIME, AND ENERGY REINFORCE EACH OTHER ——

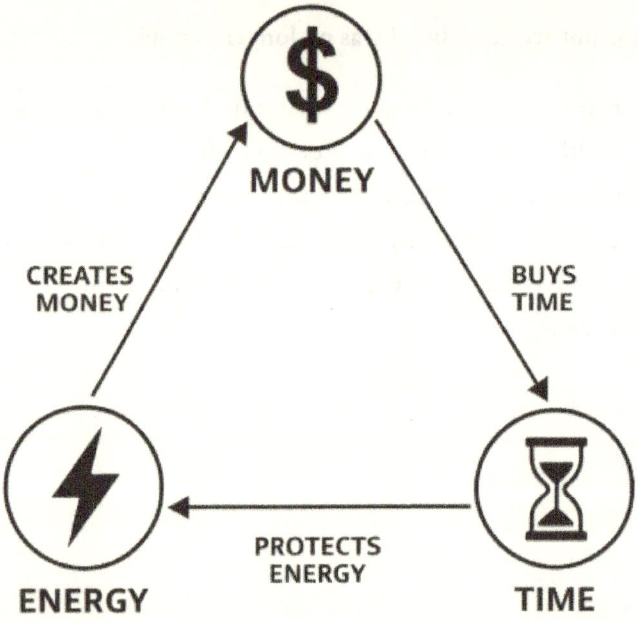

As the illustration shows, when money, time, and energy work together, financial and emotional stability compound.

Wealth is often measured only in money, but I don't think money alone creates a good life. It provides security and options, but time determines how freely you can live, while energy determines how fully you can engage with life and the people around you. When any one of these three resources is depleted, the other two lose their value.

Most people try to improve one of these aspects while unknowingly draining the other two. They earn more money, but lose time and energy. They pursue better returns, but increase complexity and stress. They optimize efficiency, but burn out in the process. Each decision may make sense on its own; but without a system, the pieces don't work together.

This is why progress feels slow, fragile, or unsustainable. This book offers a different approach. It presents a proven system for building wealth across money, time, and energy. They are separate concepts, but they work together here as interconnected parts of a structure that compound over time.

This book is not a rewrite of old wisdom. I attempt in this book to translate these timeless principles into modern life, grounding them in how people think, feel, and decide here in the 21st century. They are organized around a structure I call the **Seven Pillars of Wealth**, a set of practical foundations that strengthen step by step your financial, emotional, and inner life. They are not tricks or shortcuts, but powerful bases upon which to build.

Each pillar is simple on its own, but together they form a system designed to create financial security without sacrificing time; reduce stress by simplifying decisions; and build progress that is steady and durable.

The pillars are built on each other in sequence. We begin by creating margin to build a financial and emotional cushion. We learn to direct that margin intentionally by prioritizing what we spend it on. We then allow time to compound it. We protect what we have built. We position our housing choices wisely to support it. We then prepare for uncertainty while expanding our earning power.

The 7 Pillars Wealth Flywheel

Self-Reinforcing Wealth-Building Cycle

The chart above was designed to emphasize that small, consistent actions reinforce one another. As the cycle repeats, stability increases, fragility declines, and wealth compounds.

The ideas in this book aren't new or complicated. They are simple and proven. That is exactly why they work.

Knowing them, however, is one thing; organizing them into a structure that holds up in real life is another.

As my career has evolved, I have seen this clearly in another context, that of financial markets. There, the difference between success and failure is rarely between smart and foolish people; it is between systems that absorb stress and systems that break under it. The same is true in personal finance.

Our money decisions are never purely logical. They are shaped by emotions such as fear, urgency, guilt, pride, and confidence. When we ignore this emotional layer, we fail in practice, even if we follow good theoretical advice. When money, time, and energy are aligned, something different happens. Our financial stability improves. Our emotional pressure declines. Our progress begins to compound.

Think of this book as a set of frameworks, not prescriptions. Your situation will be different, and your path should reflect that.

If money has ever felt heavy in your hands, if progress has felt slower than it should be, or if you have done everything right and still feel uncertain, rest assured that you are not broken. You are simply missing a system. The Seven Pillars of Wealth provides that structure.

Each pillar builds on the last. Together, they reduce fragility, increase stability, and allow wealth to grow in a way that holds up over time.

The goal is not just to grow money, but to protect the time and energy that make wealth worth having. Now, let's begin.

Reader Resources

To help you apply the ideas in this book, I have created a collection of companion resources and worksheets available online for free at:

https://xufenghua.com/wealth

CHAPTER 1

PAY YOURSELF FIRST

KEEPING THE FIRST SLICE TO EARN SELF-RESPECT

"Wealth is what you don't see."
— Morgan Housel, *The Psychology of Money*[2]

Most people assume wealth is always visible. They think of large houses, expensive cars, and other obvious signs of success. The opposite, however, is usually true. The wealth that truly changes lives is often the wealth no one sees.

Earlier this century, a man named Geoffrey Holt lived quietly in a mobile home park in Hinsdale, New Hampshire. He worked as a groundskeeper there, mowing lawns and maintaining the overall property. He wore simple clothes, drove an old vehicle, and kept largely to himself. To most people in town, he looked like someone who was only just getting by.

When he passed away in 2023, however, the town discovered something unexpected. He had quietly accumulated $3.8 million, which he left to the community to support education, recreation, and local services.[3]

How does someone earning an ordinary income build that kind of wealth?

Most people assume wealth comes from high salaries, successful businesses, or lucky investment windfalls.

Geoffrey Holt had none of those advantages. What he had was something far simpler. For decades, he followed a quiet rule most people ignore: **keep the first slice**. When receiving a small but decent settlement after the closure of a grain mill where he was a manager, he invested it instead of upgrading his lifestyle. That small decision, repeated year after year with each annual dividend, created the kind of invisible wealth that most people never see.

In both my own life and later professional work, I've learned that the difficulty in building wealth is rarely mathematical. The numbers are usually clear. I find the real obstacle is emotional friction. Fear, pressure, and urgency distort decisions long before spreadsheets do.

This chapter is about that first principle, that building wealth is not about high income or clever investing. The foundation is simpler: keep part of what you earn and do so before optimizing your finances.

Financial wealth begins as emotional wealth. It starts with restraint and with margin built intentionally into the system.

Most people struggle not because they earn too little, but because their financial lives lack margin—the amount of money they have above the amount they need to pay their bills.

Paying yourself first is not just a savings tactic; it's a structural rule that changes how money behaves in your life. It creates stability before growth, and protection before progress.

It isn't just about money, but also about creating margin across three resources. It creates margin in money, which builds security. It creates margin in time, which creates flexibility. In addition, it creates margin in energy, which reduces pressure.

That margin is where everything else begins. This chapter will show you how to build that margin, one paycheck at a time.

The First Time I Paid Myself First

Long before I understood compound interest or retirement accounts, I learned this principle in a different way.

When school tuition came due the year I was nine, money was tight; my parents were away working, and my grandparents were doing their best to care for us. That week, I took out a small metal box where I would keep my allowance and holiday money when it came in. It wasn't much, but it was the first money I ever personally controlled.

I used it to pay my tuition, so my education wouldn't become a burden to my grandparents. I didn't realize it would happen, but something shifted in my mind that day.

I inherently understood, without needing it explained, a principle that would shape my life for years to come: the money I keep for emergencies shapes me more than the money I spend on frivolous things.

That's why I start with the concept of paying yourself first in the Seven Pillars framework. Keeping the first slice of what you earn changes your relationship with money. It helps you build self-respect, create margin, and separate who you are from any chaos that might be happening around you.

We all have a moment—early or late—when we realize that wealth does not begin with income. It begins the first time we set aside something for the future and decide it belongs there. For me, that moment came from a metal box at the age of nine; for you, it can begin with your very next paycheck.

The Rule of 10 Percent

Years later, I found myself in a small Brooklyn apartment. It was 2012. I had just paid rent. My bank balance was low, and I was doing the familiar math: groceries or buffer? I remember the realization clearly: if I kept living on the edge, life would keep pushing me over it.

What I organically learned as a child through necessity, I later had to relearn as an adult through deliberate structure. That night, for the first time, I drew a line between who I was and who I wanted to become.

I created a new rule for myself: 10 percent of every paycheck goes to a Future Me savings account, automated so that I didn't even have to think about it.

I didn't wait until I "felt ready," and I didn't make exceptions when things got tight. I didn't realize it then, but I wasn't just changing my budget; I was redesigning how my entire personal financial system worked.

When the first transfer happened, I didn't feel richer, but something important had shifted.

I had created margin—small but real—a buffer I had never had in my life before. That single act didn't transform my life overnight, but it did change the direction of my life immediately.

For the very first time, my savings began to grow, and my anxiety began to ease. The question that used to follow every purchase—"What if?"—no longer ran the room. I was not just surviving; I was preparing.

Every automated transfer sent the same message: I matter, my future matters, and I am willing to prove it. This is why the Rule of 10 Percent works.

What I began as a financial habit started to change something else for me. I was not only building savings, but also creating space in my time and stability in my energy.

Note that this rule is not about the amount, but rather about the identity it builds. Ten percent is not a magic number; that is a starting signal.

We can't negotiate with the principle, but we can adjust the percentage based on our circumstances. No matter what that amount is, when you keep the first slice of every dollar, you stop treating your future as an afterthought and instead start preparing for it.

The more you follow this rule, the more you get used to it, and the more solid the foundation you lay for the subsequent pillars.

Preserving Capital Before Consumption

Another winter night in New York, I got off at the wrong subway station. I checked my transit card balance and realized I could not swipe back in without risking an overdraft. So, I zipped up my jacket and walked the distance instead.

That wasn't a dramatic decision—it was only a 15-minute walk—but when you are close to empty, small choices carry a weight far beyond the literal number. That walk clarified something important to me: wealth is not about how much you earn, but whether you keep any of it.

For a long time, I lived in what I now recognize as consumption mode. Money came in and went right back out—not recklessly, but certainly without thinking about it. I had a purpose for every dollar, but none of them belonged to the future.

What I eventually realized is that wealth begins the moment you exit consumption mode and enter preservation mode. That shift requires discipline, not abundance.

It starts with a simple rule: no matter how many or how few eggs in your basket, keep one. It's that act that changes how you relate to money, not how many eggs you have in total.

When you decide that one portion of what you earn is untouchable, you stop treating money as something life takes from you. You start treating it as something you protect. That shift matters more than the amount.

Most people consume everything they earn and tell themselves they will save later—when their income rises, when their life calms down, when they can "finally afford it."

But wealth starts when behavior changes, not when conditions improve. In fact, the higher your income, the more expensive it becomes to delay this habit. Your lifestyle expands faster than your discipline if you don't protect your savings.

Keeping one egg is how you prove to yourself that the future exists and matters. This principle scales; whether you earn $500 a week or $5,000, the habit is the same. Over time, that preserved portion becomes momentum. That momentum helps you gain more confidence. As your confidence increases, you also expand your capacity.

Delay Is an Invisible Tax

Most costly decisions don't feel costly at the time. They feel small, reasonable, and easy to postpone.

When people imagine financial setbacks, they picture dramatic events, such as job losses, medical bills, and market crashes.

The most common obstacle, however, is not a crisis but a delay. Not because people are irresponsible. Not because they don't understand money. But because they delay the moment when saving becomes non-negotiable. Income does not fix this problem. Structure and margin do.

Early in my career, I told myself I would start saving and investing later—when my salary was higher, when life felt calmer, or when there was more breathing room. That logic felt sensible, but it was flawed. Time, not income, does most of the work of building wealth. The real cost of waiting is not missed dollars but missed years.

Compounding rewards those who start before they feel ready. Early contributions buy time. When saving is delayed, no amount of effort later can fully replace that lost time.

This is why two people with similar incomes and investment strategies can end up in very different places. The one with more wealth didn't make better decisions, but simply made them earlier.

That is why paying yourself first matters so much. It removes the option to delay and turns intention into action before doubt has time to intervene. You stop hoping the next raise will change things. You stop waiting for perfect conditions. Wealth begins the day that waiting ends, and when saving becomes automatic and future focused.

The Emotional Wealth Hidden in Saving

Most people think saving is about numbers. But its most powerful effect appears long before the numbers grow.

Saving changes how money feels. When you begin keeping the first slice of what you earn, something subtle shifts. The constant background tension eases. Decisions feel lighter. You aren't rich, but you are no longer fragile.

Before I saved consistently, money felt loud. Even small purchases carried weight. There was no margin to absorb mistakes. When something is set aside for the future, you stop holding your breath.

Urgency fades. Panic softens. This is the return most people underestimate.

Saving doesn't create excitement. It creates safety. Not from growth, but from margin. Margin isn't comfort; it is decision quality under pressure. When margin exists, mistakes are survivable. Choices widen. Time begins to work in your favor.

What you are really building is not just a bank account balance. You are building distance from pressure, which gives you the ability to wait, the ability to choose, and the ability to say no without fear. That is where emotional wealth begins.

Common Frictions

Barrier 1: "I have debt. Shouldn't I pay that off first?"

This is one of the most common concerns about paying yourself first, and a reasonable one.

Paying yourself first does not mean ignoring debt. It means refusing to leave your future completely unprotected while you address the past.

Even while paying down loans, setting aside a small, consistent amount builds margin, and prevents one setback from forcing you deeper into debt. A modest emergency fund prevents the shocks of taking on new high-interest debt. The principle is not the percentage. The principle is continuity.

Barrier 2: "I have nothing left over to save once I pay my bills."

When money feels tight, saving can feel unrealistic. But this is often when saving matters most.

Paying yourself first does not require large amounts. It requires a line in the sand; that no matter how small it is, something gets set aside before spending absorbs everything.

Even small, automatic transfers create proof that the future exists and deserves a claim. Over time, that proof changes behavior.

Barrier 3: "I'll start once my income is higher."

Paying yourself first is rarely a timing issue. It is usually a structural one. When income rises before savings habits are set, your spending simply expands faster. Starting to save earlier, even at a small scale, anchors the behavior before "lifestyle creep" has a chance to consume it.

The habit matters more than the amount. Wealth begins the moment you keep the first slice.

Chapter 1 Summary

- Wealth begins with a decision, not a number. Paying yourself first is the moment you claim your future before life consumes the present.

- Financial stress is rarely caused by low income. It is usually caused by living without margin. Having extra money for emergencies reduces urgency, restores choice, and changes how decisions are made under pressure.

- Waiting feels harmless, but it is actually expensive. Time rewards those who build structures early, not those who wait for perfect conditions. Starting small, even before you feel ready, is the advantage. The habit matters more than the percentage. Keeping the first slice anchors behavior before income, lifestyle, or excuses can erase it.

- Emotional wealth arrives before monetary wealth. Calm, stability, and resilience make long-term wealth possible.
- This pillar strengthens money by building financial margin, expands time by creating future flexibility, and preserves energy by reducing financial pressure.

Chapter 1 Action Plan

1. **Automate the first slice.** Automatically route money into savings before becoming tempted to spend it. Start at 10 percent if possible. If not, start smaller—but make it automatic and untouchable.

2. **Separate it physically.** Move this money to a different bank account and name it with intent (e.g., *Future Me*). What's separated survives.

3. **Create margin on purpose.** Remove or downgrade one lifestyle expense this month, so saving doesn't feel like deprivation.

4. **Observe, do not manage.** Once a week, quickly look at the Future Me balance to see the current total. No changes. No judgment. Just awareness.

5. **Do it now.** Within 24 hours of reading this chapter, complete one concrete action—set up the payroll au-

tomation, put an amount of money into savings, or skip one lifestyle expense. Momentum starts with evidence.

Paying yourself first does not solve your money problems. It reveals them. It also changes how you use your time and how you experience your energy.

Once the first slice is protected, every remaining dollar demands intention as well. The next chapter is about this intention—choosing what truly supports your life, then letting go of the rest without guilt.

Chapter 2

Prioritize Your Spending

Intentional spending brings you peace.

"You can afford anything, but not everything."
— Paula Pant, *Afford Anything*[4]

As recently profiled in *Business Insider*, in 2023, marketing professional Angelisa Cuniff was 27, living in New York City, and earning a six-figure salary. On paper, she had done everything right. She had a strong job, a solo apartment, and the freedom to travel, dine out, and enjoy the city she worked so hard to be part of. This was supposed to be the reward.

Instead, she found herself $25,000 in credit card debt. This happened not because she was reckless or ignorant. Her spending increased quietly and without much notice. She got a nicer apartment, ate out a little more often, and had a few more "this is normal now" upgrades. None of it felt dramatic. Everything felt deserved. That is why the danger went unnoticed.

Eventually, she did something uncomfortable: she downsized, cutting the expenses in her lifestyle that no longer added real value. She rebuilt the margin. Almost immediately, something changed.

She slept better. Her stress dropped. Her priorities became clearer. Her income stayed the same, but her life felt lighter.[5]

This story isn't rare; I ran straight into it early in my own career. As my income rose, so did my expenses, until the numbers started to make my life feel heavier, not lighter.

Spending does not create freedom. Priorities do. When spending isn't decided in advance, income disappears without direction. Every expense is a tradeoff across three resources. We spend money, commit time, and use our energy. When our priorities are unclear, all three are consumed without intention.

The lesson was unavoidable: income does not create ease. Margin does. It appears when spending decisions are made intentionally.

When Every Dollar Carries Weight

When money feels tight, it is rarely because you are spending irresponsibly. More often, it is because you have not defined your priorities in advance.

Early in my career, every dollar I spent carried weight. It wasn't because I lacked discipline; it was because I hadn't defined what really mattered in my life. Without clear priorities, each purchase triggered the same question: is this the right choice for me? When every spending decision feels like a blind guess, money becomes exhausting. That is the hidden cost of unintentional spending; it turns money into constant negotiation.

What I eventually learned is simple but uncomfortable. You do not need to control every dollar; you need to control the ones that matter most.

This is where the well-known 80/20 rule applies to spending—roughly 80 percent of your satisfaction in life comes from about 20 percent of your expenses. If you don't identify that critical 20 percent, everything competes for attention, which means everything feels equally important.

Unintentional spending flattens priorities. Intentional spending restores a hierarchy. Once I began treating spending as a hierarchy instead of a bullet point list, the pressure eased. I put needs first, then chose a small number of high-value wants deliberately. The goal was not deprivation; it was alignment.

When you decide in advance what deserves your money, spending becomes lighter. Guilt fades. You stop replaying decisions. You stop having buyer's remorse. You don't confuse earning more with living better.

I faced a simple decision at home a couple of years ago. I could mow the lawn myself. That meant buying equipment, setting aside time each week, and handling the upkeep. Or I could hire a landscaping company for about $100 a month. Doing it myself would save money.

But the tradeoff was not just financial. Time that could be spent with my daughter would be replaced by chores. Energy that could go toward more meaningful work would be used for maintenance.

I chose to outsource it. Yes, I spent money, but I reclaimed time and preserved energy. Not every decision should be optimized for cost. You should optimize some for how you live.

Lifestyle Creep Doesn't Ask for Permission

Lifestyle creep rarely announces itself as a mistake. Instead, it arrives disguised as progress.

We work hard and we earn more. Life finally feels a little easier. So, understandably, we make upgrades to our lifestyle. We choose a slightly bigger apartment than we need. We pick a neighborhood for how it sounds, not how it lives. We make upgrades that look impressive but don't make Tuesday any better. Those changes feel normal. They feel like things we deserve for all our hard work.

That is exactly why lifestyle creep is dangerous. It doesn't feel like overspending; it feels like success.

Awareness alone doesn't stop it, because lifestyle creep isn't driven by ignorance, but by default decisions embedded in daily life. When spending decisions are not clearly and intentionally defined, they default to what feels appropriate in the moment. Income rises, expectations rise with it, and expenses steadily expand to fill the space. No single choice stands out.

The damage is not in one decision; it's accumulated.

I ran into this early in my career. Once after a raise, I moved from a shared apartment into a studio, doubling my rent. On paper, it made sense. I could afford it. It felt more adult. It made me proud. And part of it, if I am being honest, was wanting my life to look to others like it was moving forward. And it did, but what didn't move forward was my sense of ease.

My savings began shrinking month after month, even though my income was higher. I didn't feel anything was broken, or that I was doing anything wrong. I wasn't splurging, nor was I being careless. That's the nature of lifestyle creep; it raises our floor without raising our safety.

After a few months, I did something uncomfortable: I ended the lease and moved into a much cheaper place. It wasn't glamorous, but the effect on my wealth was immediate. My savings recovered. I felt less stressed. My priorities became clearer.

That decision didn't make my life smaller. It made my life more workable.

Lifestyle creep erodes future wealth more reliably than bad investments ever could. We cannot out-earn undisciplined spending. Neither do raises alone fix drift.

Wealth lives in the gap between what we earn and what we keep, which we must protect deliberately. It does not grow by accident. If you do not protect it, spending erases it.

The Permission-Based Budget

When spending decisions are made by default, drift is inevitable. The only way to stop drift is to decide on your spending in advance. That is where a permission-based budget comes in.

Most people think of a budget as a cage, a list of things they're not allowed to do. They think of the spreadsheets that are designed to enforce discipline through restriction. That framing makes budgeting fail.

A permission-based budget works in the opposite direction. This is not about tracking; it is about making fewer decisions in the heat of the moment, because the system instead decides for you in advance.

The goal is not to monitor spending after it happens. It is to remove decision-making *before* spending happens. When priorities are clear, money stops demanding constant attention.

Instead of asking, *"What should I cut?"* a permission-based budget starts with a better question: *"What actually matters?"* We decide ahead of time which categories deserve our money, and which don't. Once those decisions are made, spending becomes simpler. We spend freely where it matters.

You decide ahead of time which categories deserve your money and which don't. Once those decisions are made, spending becomes simpler. You spend freely where it matters.

A simple way to make this practical is to define three categories: what you value most (spend freely), what you don't value (cut aggressively), and everything else (keep simple and contained). Clarity in these three areas helps you remove most day-to-day friction.

This is not about optimizing every dollar or winning a frugality contest. It is about restoring hierarchy. Most of our personal satisfaction in life comes from only a few categories. Once we protect those, the rest categories lose power against us.

One example of this in practice was when my spouse and I upgraded our family car after having a child. We chose a larger and safer vehicle, even though it meant paying more each month on the lease. Safety and reliability were priorities, and we decided that in advance. Because the decision was intentional and built into the system, it didn't create stress or second-guessing. That's the difference permission makes.

For me, this shift was subtle but powerful. I stopped trying to be "good with money" in every single aspect of my life. Once I decided what spending truly improved my life—spending that improved stability, health, time, and education—the rest became easier to ignore. Cutting stopped feeling arbitrary.

A permission-based budget does not make our life smaller. It makes it deliberate. **We regain control not by saying no more often, but by saying yes with purpose.** Drift requires indecision. Design removes it. That is the role of a permission-based budget: to turn intention into structure, so drift doesn't get a vote.

When Spending Locks In

Two people make the same income. One feels in control. The other feels stuck. The difference is not how much they earn, but what they have already committed to. This is not about how much we spend. It is about how much of our spending is locked in.

Not all spending works the same way. Some costs are flexible, while others are locked.

Flexible spending moves up and down. Dining out, travel, and hobbies can expand in good times and shrink when needed. On the other hand, things like rent, car payments, insurance, and streaming subscriptions repeat every month. Lifestyle creep often hides here, quietly turning choices into obligations.

I saw this in my own life. Early in my career, I lived alone in a studio for about $1,100 a month. My girlfriend, now my wife, would come over on weekends. Later, I rented a room in a shared house for around $500. I had the same job, in the same city, for the same income, but everything felt different.

In the studio, a large part of my income was already spoken for before I even received it. I had less room to save, invest, or absorb surprises, whereas in the shared house, that pressure eased. I cut rent in half to create margin without changing my income. That margin showed up everywhere. I started to save more consistently. I invested earlier. I felt less stress when expenses came up.

Flexible spending affects comfort. Fixed spending affects stability. When income falls, flexible spending can change, but fixed costs cannot. When too much of our life becomes fixed, our margin shrinks quietly. We have less room for errors. We feel it when we hesitate to take risks or delay decisions.

Flexibility is a quiet form of wealth. The more we fix, the less we can flex. Wealth is not only the ability to spend. It is the ability to adjust.

The Emotional Wealth of Intentionality

Intentional spending changes how money feels long before it changes how much we have. When spending is deliberate, money stops becoming constant background noise. We no longer react emotionally to bills or impulses. We are choosing. That shift, from reaction to intention, is where emotional wealth begins.

Before I learned to spend intentionally, even small purchases felt heavy. Every decision carried uncertainty because priorities had not been set in advance. When money has no direction, every dollar feels like a guess.

Intentionality removes that friction. When we know what our money is for, we can enjoy spending without second-guessing it. We can also say no calmly without resentment to what doesn't matter. That is because the decision has already been made. We are not depriving ourselves. That creates a different kind of emotional wealth: confidence.

We stop renegotiating decisions after the fact. We trust our choices because they align with our priorities. **Emotional control is not about feeling calm all the time; it's about knowing one imperfect decision will not undo years of progress.**

Spending discipline is not a restraint for its own sake. It is what preserves what we have already protected.

Common Frictions

Barrier 1: "I don't want to feel deprived."

This is rarely about money. It's about identity.

Your feeling of deprivation comes from unclear priorities, not from limits. When you give in to every temptation to spend money, every decision becomes a negotiation. When you choose a few things deliberately, however, the rest lose their pull on you.

Intentional spending is not about saying no more often. It is about saying yes with purpose. This is not about spending less. It's about deciding what deserves your resources, so the rest stops competing for your attention.

Barrier 2: "I'll start prioritizing spending once my income is higher."

This is rarely a timing issue. It's a structural one.

When income rises, spending rises with it. It may not rise all at once, but it occurs through small upgrades that feel reasonable.

Before long, much of your income is already spoken for. The issue is not how much you earn. It is how much flexibility you keep in your life. If priorities are not set early, higher income reinforces existing patterns instead of improving them. Income can improve your life, but structure determines whether it actually does.

Barrier 3: "Tracking every expense feels exhausting."

That is because tracking is not the solution.

Intentional spending works by making general decisions in advance. Once priorities are clear, most needs for making decisions disappear, and thus the need for tracking these decisions disappears as well. The system does the work for you rather than relying on your willpower.

Clarity reduces your effort. Your gain of control comes from design, not attention.

Chapter 2 Summary

- Spending is emotional before it is mathematical. When priorities are undefined, every dollar carries weight, and decision fatigue accumulates.
- Lifestyle creep is not recklessness; it is drift. As income

rises, spending expands steadily unless structure intervenes.

- Margin is preserved not by restriction, but by hierarchy. Deciding in advance what matters prevents leakage.
- Intentional spending restores control. Guilt fades when decisions are pre-made and aligned with values.
- Emotional wealth appears early. Calm replaces negotiation when money has direction.
- This pillar strengthens money by directing spending toward what matters, frees up time by reducing decision fatigue and misalignment, and preserves energy by removing friction and ongoing financial stress.

Chapter 2 Action Plan

1. **Begin tracking your spending.** Observe one full month of spending without making any corrections yet. Data first. Judgment later.
2. **Identify the 20 percent that matters.** Circle the few categories that create most of your satisfaction. Everything else is optional noise.
3. **Write your spending permissions.** Literally write it on a piece of paper, or in a text document. Decide where you spend freely and where you don't. Clarity replaces restraint.
4. **Eliminate one low-value cost.** Cut, downgrade, or

pause a recurring expense that adds little life value.

5. **Lock decisions in advance.** Turn priorities into structure so fewer choices are required in the moment.

Our savings create margin. We preserve it through intentional spending.

The next pillar is about putting our protected capital to work—patiently, deliberately, and without turning progress into pressure. That is where money begins to grow, time begins to matter, and energy is conserved.

Chapter 3

Power Your Savings

Investing builds momentum.

"The first rule of compounding: never interrupt it unnecessarily."
— Charlie Munger [6]

Compounding is often described as a mathematical advantage. In practice, it is a behavioral one. It only works when savings are protected and left alone. It works across three resources. We grow money. Time does the work. We preserve energy by not interfering.

Compounding is not guaranteed. It depends on where the money is placed. Cash compounds slowly and predictably. Investments compound unevenly, with periods of decline along the way. In this book, compounding refers to letting savings grow over time—through uncertainty, not in spite of it.

Anne Scheiber never earned much money. She spent most of her career as an IRS auditor, lived alone in a small apartment, and kept her life simple. She wore the same coats year after year, avoided luxuries, and rarely drew attention to herself. When she passed away at 101, the world was stunned to learn she had accumulated more than $22 million.[7]

Compounding isn't powerful because of math; it is powerful because it rewards those who can leave progress alone long enough for time to take control.

For Scheiber, there was no inheritance, no business empire, no lucky break. She didn't speculate or chase trends. Instead, she invested steadily in a small number of strong companies, reinvested every dividend, and rarely sold. Then she waited. She allowed time to do the work she never tried to rush.

What makes her story powerful is not how extraordinary it is, but how ordinary it looks. She didn't predict recessions or outsmart Wall Street. She understood a simple truth: money grows the most profoundly when it is left alone long enough to compound.

That patience is uncomfortable. In the early years, progress might be invisible. There are periods when doubt will creep in, when nothing seems to be happening.

Most people interrupt it at that stage, but Scheiber kept her money invested. Her wealth was not built by doing more. It was built by doing less but doing it consistently. She didn't confuse activity with progress, or demand constant feedback. She let the system run without interference.

That same force—slow, patient, and relentless—is available to anyone. We don't need perfect timing; we just need consistency, time, and the discipline to stay out of our own way.

That is the heart of this chapter: how to put our savings to work, and how to let them keep working.

When My Money Started Working for Me

In 2017, when I had finally built up my emergency fund to a satisfactory number, and had enough extra money to start investing, I expected something big to happen.

Instead, in the first month, my tax-free retirement account actually went down by 75 cents. The following month, it was up by only nine dollars. In the third month, it increased by a mere 79 cents.

The numbers felt small, almost insulting, especially after all the effort it had taken to save that money. It felt disappointing. I remember wondering whether I was doing something wrong or wasting my time. But I stayed consistent. I kept contributing. I didn't tinker or chase speculation.

Years later, when I finally had a chance to zoom out and see the big picture, the system told a different story. From June 2017 to January 2026, that retirement account posted a cumulative return of 170.23%. What looked like failure at the beginning was simply early progress.

These results were achieved over a strong market period. The path will not always look like this, but the principle remains the same: consistency matters more than timing.

Most people never experience this satisfactory long view of investing, not because they can't do it, but because they quit too soon. We are wired to expect immediate results, especially here in the US. The real work in compounding, though, happens before it becomes visible, adding up beneath the surface while we live our lives.

That was another moment my relationship with money changed. It was now something working alongside me—while I slept, while I studied, while I focused on my career and my family, even when I did nothing. This is the power of long-term investing: our money starts working on its own without our help, while we focus on simply living our lives.

What I've shared here is not a guide to selecting investments, but a framework to ensure whatever you choose has time to work and to compound.

When Compounding Looks Weak

Albert Einstein is often credited with calling compound interest the eighth wonder of the world. Whether he said it matters less than why the statement endures.

Compounding does not fail in the early years; it simply fails to impress. That distinction matters.

Most people don't abandon compounding because it performs poorly; they abandon it because it doesn't look meaningful at the beginning. Early results feel small relative to the patience required. Progress is easy to overlook. From the outside, it resembles stagnation. From the inside, it feels inefficient.

This is not a flaw, however; it's a structural feature of the ever-increasing curve defined by exponential growth. In the beginning, returns are driven more by contributions than by growth. Time has not accumulated enough mass to matter. Compounding has not yet taken over. What looks slow is often building.

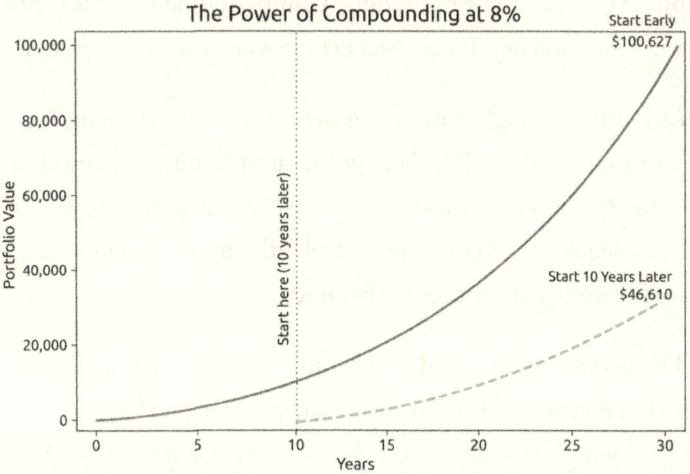

The above simple chart shows two investors saving the same way, with one starting ten years earlier and achieving much greater long-term growth. They both begin in the same way, and they both represent the same habits and the same amount of seed money. The only difference is when they start.

At first, the gap between the two is small, easy to ignore. It doesn't feel decisive. Then time begins to separate them. The earlier returns start compounding on themselves. The later start has less time to build. The distance grows quietly at first, then becomes dramatic all at once.

One way to make compounding visible is the Rule of 72; take the number 72 and divide by your annual rate of return, and you get a rough estimate of how many years it takes for your money to double. At 8 percent, it is about nine years. At 6 percent, it is twelve. At 12 percent, it is six.

But even this can be misleading. Compounding rewards consistency, not urgency. It penalizes people when they are impatient.

Early on, I thought improving my returns meant doing more: adjusting positions, hopping on the latest trends, reacting faster, trying to guess right more often. It felt productive, but over time I noticed something uncomfortable: the more I interfered, the more inconsistent the results became.

The periods that worked best for me were not when I was most active; they were when I made a good decision and left it alone.

Compounding does not need constant input; it needs uninterrupted time. Every unnecessary change resets the process. Every reaction introduces friction.

The real threat isn't low returns; it is interruption.

An investor might start with a great simple plan. They invest consistently and keep their investments diversified. At first, it works exactly like it should. Then suddenly the markets take a temporary fall. Fear rises. They sell. The markets recover. They buy back in, but now at a higher price than before. Their returns shrink because their investment was interrupted.

The strategy didn't fail; it was their behavior that changed the outcome.

Warren Buffett's late business partner, Charlie Munger, reminded us that compounding doesn't require brilliance; it requires restraint. Small, repeated actions, left to their own devices, eventually dominate outcomes. The hardest part isn't starting; it's not interrupting.

That is the discipline this chapter builds toward—not doing more, but learning when not to interfere.

Where Compounding Lives

Leaving compounding alone is one part of the equation; where you place your money is the other. Not all compounding is the same. *Where* our money grows matters just as much as *how*.

There are three broad types of accounts your savings can live in: taxable, tax-deferred, and tax-free.

- In a taxable account, gains are taxed along the way. Dividends, interest, and realized gains create a steady drag. Compounding still works, but part of the return is removed by taxes before it can build on itself.

- In a tax-deferred account, taxes are postponed. Gains are not taxed each year, allowing more of the return to remain invested and compound. The trade-off comes later when withdrawals are taxed.

- In a tax-free account, gains are not taxed at all. Compounding works without interruption, and what accumulates is fully retained.

The difference between the three types of accounts may seem small in a single year; but over time, it becomes meaningful.

Compounding is sensitive to friction. Even a small, recurring tax slows the rate at which capital builds. The effect isn't linear; it compounds.

Two portfolios earning the same pre-tax return can end up in very different places simply because one faced less friction along the way. It isn't about avoiding taxes entirely; it's about placing the right assets in the right environment, so compounding can work with fewer interruptions.

Taxable accounts offer flexibility. Tax-deferred accounts offer time. Tax-free accounts offer efficiency. Each has a role. But over a long enough period, the accounts that minimize ongoing drag tend to do more of the heavy lifting.

Compounding doesn't just depend on returns; it depends on how much of those returns you are allowed to keep.

Our goal is not to have complex strategies, but to align the compounding with the correct accounts. Let compounding work in environments where it is disrupted the least.

Don't Expect the Market to Love You

Understanding compounding is easy. Allowing it to work—without interference—is where most people fail.

A common mistake that investors make is assuming the market will reward participation rather than discipline. It does not. The market doesn't care about effort, intention, or confidence. It doesn't respond to how badly you want to be right. It moves on its own terms.

I learned this lesson the hard way. In 2018, I opened a tax-free retirement account with a small initial deposit. Early results were strong. The account grew quickly, and I took that growth as confirmation. I assumed it was because of my skills. I believed the market was responding to my intelligence and effort.

That belief turned out to be the problem. When the results turned, they didn't just reverse; they eroded. I responded by trading even more, reacting faster, and pushing harder. By the end of the following year, most of the money in the account was gone.

The financial loss hurt, but the more serious damage was internal.

I confused luck with ability, and mistakenly considered activity as progress. Short-term success proved dangerous. What I should have done instead was stay invested, keep my trading costs low, and let time do the work for me, instead of trying to force outcomes through my own perceived cleverness.

When we need excitement in our lives, we tend to trade more. When we need validation, we take risks we don't understand. But don't expect the market to love us for these things; expect it to test our patience. Those who pass that test don't look clever at the moment; they look boring. Over time, boring wins.

One reason compounding is so hard to trust is that luck dominates short-term investing.

Early results say very little about skill. Good decisions can lose money, and bad decisions can look brilliant. Over time, behavior takes over discipline. The reason compounding works is not because it eliminates luck, but because it makes luck irrelevant if we stay invested long enough.

The Emotional Wealth of Watching Growth

Watching your money grow rarely feels dramatic. It is slow, uneven, and often unremarkable.

Because when compounding is working, it doesn't announce itself or reward you with reassurance, it simply accumulates. Over time, that steady accumulation changes something more important than your balance. It changes how effort, risk, and time are experienced.

For years, money felt like something I had to push uphill. If I wasn't actively doing something—earning, optimizing, checking, adjusting—I felt exposed. Progress felt uncertain.

Compounding dismantled that belief. As my investments began to grow, even modestly, I noticed the shift in my behavior before I noticed it in the numbers. Anxiety didn't disappear, but it did soften. Mistakes felt survivable.

That change didn't come from big wins. It came from consistency—watching small contributions continue to work without my involvement, and seeing time absorb volatility instead of amplifying it.

This is the emotional wealth that compounding creates. When growth becomes steady instead of dramatic, our nervous systems adapt. We stop chasing reassurance. We stop mistaking movement for progress. Our patience emerges not as a personality trait, but as a byproduct of structure.

The reward of long-term investing is not excitement or validation but relief. When compounding is allowed to work, our future stops feeling unstable. It starts to feel durable.

Common Frictions

Barrier 1: "Nothing seems to be happening."

This is not a performance issue. It is a visibility issue.

Early compounding is dominated by contributions, not growth. Progress exists, but it does not announce itself.

Compounding works before it looks like it works.

Barrier 2: "I'll invest once I feel more confident about my investment choices."

This is rarely about knowledge. It is about reassurance.

Confidence usually arrives after results, not before them. Waiting for certainty delays the very process that creates it. Early investing feels uncomfortable because feedback is weak.

Consistency builds confidence, not the other way around.

Barrier 3: "I can do better if I'm more active."

This is overestimating your control of the situation.

Markets reward behavior over brilliance. Most investors don't lose because they lack intelligence; they lose because they interrupt processes that were already working.

The edge comes from restraint, not reaction.

Chapter 3 Summary

- Compounding isn't a math problem; it's a behavioral one. Time rewards consistency, not activity.
- Early progress feels weak because compounding hasn't taken over yet. Most people quit during this phase.
- Interruption is the real enemy. Panic, tinkering, and overreaction reset the clock.
- The market rewards restraint, not brilliance. Staying invested matters more than timing or prediction.
- Emotional wealth grows alongside capital. Reduced urgency makes patience possible.
- This pillar strengthens money by allowing returns to compound over time, makes time the primary driver of growth, and preserves energy by reducing the need for constant action and decision-making.

Chapter 3 Action Plan

1. **Automate your contributions.** Investing should happen without motivation, timing, or emotion.
2. **Define your "do nothing" rules.** Write down when you will *not* act—no panic selling, no trend chasing.
3. **Limit your visibility.** Check investment balances only quarterly, even only annually if you have the discipline. Less watching equals less interference.

4. **Simplify your holdings.** Favor diversified, low-cost investments over complex strategies that invite tinkering.

5. **Measure your consistency, not your returns.** Judge success by time invested and contributions made, not short-term performance.

Compounding rewards patience, but patience alone doesn't guarantee durability. Money grows. Time compounds. But without protection, both can be undone. Once progress begins, the real risk shifts from growth to fragility.

The next pillar is about protecting our savings so one mistake, one shock, or one bad year doesn't undo what time has built for us over decades.

Chapter 4

Protect Your Savings

Manage risk carefully and exercise good judgment.

"The risk of ruin is fundamentally different from other types of risk."

— Nassim Nicholas Taleb, *Fooled by Randomness*[8]

For a brief moment, Long Term Capital Management looked like a financial genius.

The firm was built by some of the most respected minds in finance, including Nobel Prize winners. Its strategy focused on small price differences across similar securities, structured to profit regardless of market direction, and relied on enormous leverage to earn meaningful returns of capital, borrowing heavily to scale its positions.[9]

Their returns were strong. Investors' confidence grew. Capital flooded in. It looked safe until it wasn't—just one year after winning the Nobel, it should be added—but by then it was too late.

What failed wasn't intelligence; it was protection.

The strategy worked as long as the markets behaved like they were supposed to. It depended on mathematical relationships between different financial instruments holding together, regardless of market conditions. Leverage amplified the gains, but it also amplified the losses once they began.

When the markets changed in 1998, their positions moved together. Losses spread. Liquidity vanished. What looked controlled became exposed. Within months, one of the most sophisticated firms in finance required a $3.6 billion rescue to prevent broader market damage.[10]

The models were sound, but the system was too fragile. Intelligence alone does not protect against fragility.

Most financial failures do not look like failures at the beginning. They look disciplined. They look consistent. They look like success. The danger isn't in taking risks; it's when growth comes before protection. Success builds confidence. Confidence reduces caution. Reduced caution exposes the downside.

Markets don't reward effort, and they don't reward intelligence. They respond to exposure.

When protection is missing, time stops helping and starts to work against us. People rarely lose wealth from bad ideas. They often lose money when they don't have protection built into their investment process.

Protection works across three resources. It helps preserve money, extend time, and protect energy from decisions made under pressure.

Compounding only works if you survive long enough to experience it. Survival is not just financial. It is the ability to stay in the game—over time, and without losing the judgment needed to continue.

This chapter is about protecting what works before success makes protection feel unnecessary.

When Judgment Breaks, Capital Follows

Early in my career, something about investing started to confuse me.

The largest losses I saw among my peers didn't come from them being uneducated or uninformed. They came from these people reacting to things they shouldn't have. They jumped into risky investments, lent money out of guilt, trusted the wrong partners, or tried to recover losses too quickly.

The money lost was painful, because losses hurt twice: first when the money leaves your account, and then again when your confidence leaves with it.

Once confidence is damaged, decision quality usually deteriorates with it. As with most of the lessons in this book, I learned this personally long before I could explain it clearly to others.

There was a period when my investments were doing better than expected. Confidence came easily. Decisions felt obvious.

Then conditions changed. I tried to fix the loss. What followed wasn't a dramatic collapse, but rather a quiet erosion of trust in my own judgment. From that point on, every decision carried extra emotional weight.

Once confidence cracks, people rarely respond calmly. Some freeze. Others overcorrect. Ego disguises risk-taking as courage, adding size, increasing leverage, or refusing to cut losses when backing down feels like failure.

The most dangerous losses don't come from ignorance. They come from moments when confidence outruns caution.

We can recover from slow progress. So can we recover from missed opportunities.

Distorted judgment, however, knocks people out of the game by turning manageable losses into unrecoverable ones. Most financial damage doesn't start with a bad idea. It starts with a human reaction.

Incentives, Advice, and Misplaced Trust

Everyone has advice, especially about money. What to buy. What to sell. What we "cannot miss."

It is constantly shouted at us from cable television, finance subreddits, and our well-meaning uncle over a holiday dinner. Advice flows freely because it costs nothing to give, and sometimes randomly pays well to distribute.

A simple rule has protected me more than any clever strategy: **treat advice like advertising until the giver's incentives are clearly understood.**

In December 2022, the US Securities and Exchange Commission brought criminal charges against eight social media influencers connected to a $100 million stock-manipulation scheme promoted through Discord and Twitter (now X). These influencers didn't succeed because they were brilliant analysts. They succeeded because they first built trust, community, and confidence—then used that trust to move thinly traded stocks for their own benefit.[11]

What is unsettling is not that people fell for it, but that many of them were smart, educated, and skeptical in other areas of life.

The scheme worked by exploiting social proof and perceived authority. When the messenger sounds confident and everyone else seems convinced, doubt can feel like ignorance. That pressure silences caution before it ever gets a voice.

That is why free advice is often the most expensive kind. If we listen to that advice, we don't pay upfront, but rather with the outcomes of our decisions.

Before acting on someone's financial advice, ask three questions:

- What are their incentives?
- Can they prove that they have succeeded with their own money over time?
- What happens to me if this goes wrong—and can I survive it?

If someone profits from our excitement, they are not advising us; they are running a business that is based on tricking us.

Wisdom moves differently. Slower. Given with less certainty and urgency. It never asks us to blindly trust it. Protecting our wealth begins with protecting our judgment.

Hidden Risks in Familiar Structures

The biggest threats to wealth rarely look dangerous at first. They arrive disguised as opportunity, sophistication, or common sense.

I learned this lesson early in life watching my father build businesses—a truck operation, a chopstick factory, a bamboo sheet factory, and later a furniture shop.

None of his decisions was reckless. Every step felt logical. His ventures looked like progress. The risk was in his structure: debt obligations, thin margins, dependence on partners, and the assumption that good conditions would continue indefinitely. Complexity crept in gradually. Risk hid behind the scale.

That pattern shows up everywhere in finance. Complexity is one of the most common hidden threats. Complex investments sound smart and professional, but complexity often hides risk.

The harder it is to explain something, the easier we can misunderstand it. If we can't state to ourselves in plain terms how something makes money, how it loses money, and what breaks when conditions change, we don't own it—we're borrowing confidence from someone else.

The most dangerous phrase in finance is "I understand the risk," because it's often said right before the risk changes.

Fees are another silent drain. One or two percent feels small in a year; but over decades, it compounds to a material amount.

That said, not all fees are wasteful. For many people, paying for advice, structure, or tax efficiency helps them stay invested and make better decisions. The cost is not the problem. Misalignment is. Fees become a drag when they are paid without improving behavior, outcomes, or discipline.

Then there are emotional transactions—buying because something feels exciting, selling because something feels scary. These decisions don't feel irrational in the moment; they feel urgent. But urgency is usually the enemy of good judgment.

Protection doesn't require paranoia, but it does require clarity. We should avoid what we don't understand, be skeptical of complexity, and keep costs low.

Growth Without Protection Is Not Progress

Growth is exciting, but protection is essential. The truth is simple: wealth is not about how fast you grow; it is about how long you stay in the game.

I learned this the hard way. In 2018, I opened a brokerage account with $250. Within six months, aggressive option trades had pushed the balance close to $5,000. My confidence surged. I felt like my skills mattered more than my patience.

Then the market turned. By mid-2019, the account had fallen significantly. At that point, I still had about $2,000 in the account, and I still had the chance to exit with a nice profit. Instead, my focus shifted to recovery, and I began taking more and more risks to try to get back to the earlier $5,000. By the end of the year, the account was almost wiped out.

The market didn't destroy that account; I did, by abandoning protection when emotion began to dictate exposure.

Emotion didn't change what it was that I was investing in; it changed how big I went and how long I would go before stopping. Position sizes grew. Risk limits blurred. Losses that should have been survivable became structural. Not because the strategy changed, but because my behavior did.

This is the math many people ignore: that if we lose 50 percent, we need a 100 percent gain just to break even. Once our capital is damaged, our emotional decision-making deteriorates.

Protection is not avoiding risk; it is avoiding ruin. This is not about eliminating risk; it's about making sure no single decision can take you out of the game.

High income may help you recover financially, but it doesn't restore your damaged judgment. **Protection keeps you in the game long enough for compounding to matter.**

If everything above feels abstract, here is what protection looks like in practice:

1. Never risk what you cannot recover. A single decision should not undo years of progress.

2. Size your decisions so mistakes are survivable. Being wrong is a regular part of the process. Staying in the game is the goal.

3. Avoid decisions made under pressure. Emotion changes exposure more than it changes ideas.

4. Build margin before pursuing growth. Stability is what allows growth to last.

5. Treat loans and especially leverage with respect, not as an assumed convenience. What accelerates gains can accelerate losses faster.

These rules are simple. They are also easy to ignore when things are going well.

That is when they matter most. They do more than protect capital. They also preserve time by preventing setbacks that require years to recover, and preserve energy by reducing the need for reactive decisions under stress. Over time, following these rules becomes less about discipline and more about judgment.

The Emotional Wealth of Discernment

Discernment is one of the most valuable—and least discussed—forms of wealth. It is the ability to say no without regret. To walk away from opportunities that feel rushed. To decline certainty when uncertainty is being disguised.

Early on, many people confuse discernment with fear. But discernment isn't about avoiding risk. It's about staying in the game long enough for good decisions to compound, and bad ones to be survivable.

Every investor eventually learns two lessons: how to make money, and how to keep it. The second lesson usually arrives only after you are hurt by the first one. After losses, discernment deepens. You begin to recognize patterns. You see how urgency bypasses judgment.

Over time, discernment delivers something rare: self-trust. Not bravado. Not overconfidence. A calm confidence built on restraint.

At that stage, money stops being a source of anxiety, and starts becoming a tool you use deliberately. You no longer need to chase every opportunity or prove anything through returns.

That restraint compounds—slowly and powerfully over time.

Common Frictions

Barrier 1: "I understand the risk."

This is often familiarity mistaken for control.

Understanding how something works under normal conditions is not the same as understanding how it breaks under stress. Many failures occur not because the risk was unknown, but because it changes when pressure arrives.

If you can't explain what happens when things go wrong, then you don't understand the risk.

Barrier 2: "I don't want to miss out."

This is rarely about opportunity. It's about social pressure.

There's a reason that one of the most well-known slang phrases in the age of social media is FOMO, or "Fear of Missing Out."

Urgency compresses judgment. When others seem confident or successful, hesitation feels like weakness. But speed increases exposure before protection is in place.

Missing an upside is recoverable. Missing protection often isn't.

Barrier 3: "Being cautious will limit my growth."

This confuses restraint with fear.

Protection doesn't eliminate risk—it makes risk survivable. Growth without safeguards feels fast until one mistake permanently shrinks your base.

Staying in the game matters more than winning quickly.

Chapter 4 Summary

- Most financial losses are emotional before they are financial. Judgment fails before capital does.
- Growth without protection creates fragility. Avoiding ruin matters more than maximizing upside.
- Complexity hides risk. If you can't explain how something can fail, you don't control it.
- Advice follows incentives. Free advice often carries the highest hidden cost.
- Discernment compounds. The ability to say no calmly protects both money and confidence.
- This pillar strengthens money by preventing permanent loss and avoiding ruin, extend time by extending our ability to stay in the game, preserve energy by protecting judgment and reducing reactive decisions.

Chapter 4 Action Plan

1. **Audit your downside first.** For every asset or obligation you currently have, or are thinking of taking on, ask: *What breaks if this goes wrong?*

2. **Set loss limits in advance.** Never move them under stress.

3. **Eliminate what you don't understand.** If you can't explain how it loses money, reduce or exit.

4. **Create a personal Never list.** Pre-reject leverage, hot tips, rushed deals, and promises of guaranteed returns. Protection is not built through one large gamble; it is built through small acts of restraint repeated over time.

5. **Regularly practice deliberate restraint.** Say no to one tempting financial decision this month. Relief is the proof that you avoided unnecessary risk.

Protecting your savings keeps you in the game. It preserves money, extends time, and protects the energy needed to make clear decisions. But eventually, money meets real life, and specifically the need to have a roof over your head.

The next pillar is about positioning your housing wisely, so shelter becomes a foundation for stability, not a source of fragility.

Chapter 5

Position Your Housing Wisely

Wise housing creates stability and grounding.

"I'm happy [in my modest home]. I'd move if I thought I'd be happier someplace else."

— Warren Buffett [12]

Warren Buffett emphasizes patience, discipline, and risk management when selecting housing, often noting that a home's greatest value lies in stability and utility rather than its ability to generate outsized financial returns.

Housing works across three resources. It commits money. It can constrain or free up time. It can protect energy or consume energy through ongoing pressure.

Most people make their biggest financial decision without treating it like one.

Housing is often approached as simply another milestone or investment, but it is the decision that quietly shapes every other financial outcome. It is a positioning decision that shapes everything that follows.

In 1958, the 28-year-old Buffett bought a modest five-bedroom house in Omaha for $31,500. At the time, he was already a successful investor. He could have afforded something larger, newer, or more impressive. He chose this house anyway.

More than sixty years later, he remains in that same house, despite his wealth now being in excess of $140 billion.

Buffett has never described his home as a great investment.

Its value is simpler. It provides stability, predictable costs, and freedom from pressure. It is a place where life can happen without constant adjustment. It's in this house where he has settled routines, where he has shared meals with family and friends at the same table.

They celebrate the holidays in the same rooms each year. It also has a room for him to enjoy reading books.

Housing is not primarily a growth decision. It is a positioning decision.

Sometimes that position is renting. Sometimes it is owning. What matters is whether your housing supports stability rather than pressure to perform.

Buffett's wealth was not fueled by the return on his house. It was protected by him exercising restraint about his house. By keeping his housing simple, he preserved margin everywhere else. That margin allowed the rest of his life to compound.

Most people approach housing from the opposite direction. They treat it as a signal of success, a benchmark of arrival. Housing mistakes rarely come from numbers. They come from comparison. In doing so, people load their lives with fixed costs and pressure.

The bigger the housing commitment, the smaller the margin. The smaller the margin, the harder it becomes to think clearly. Flexibility disappears.

This chapter reverses that logic. Housing is not a signal. It is a stabilizer. Sometimes that stabilizer is a well-positioned rental. Sometimes it is a carefully purchased home. The goal is not ownership. It is control.

When housing supports you instead of stretching you, you can afford to take smarter risks elsewhere because your foundation is not fragile.

Wealth grows best on stable ground. To understand why housing deserves this level of care, we need to look at what kind of decision it really is.

Housing Is a Positioning Decision

My wife and I started our own home search in 2016. Before that, we had spent years renting. It gave us flexibility while our careers and savings were still in their early stages.

Eventually our finances improved, yet our living situation still felt temporary. Rent increased. Leases weren't renewed. Decisions were ultimately made by someone else. We wanted a place where life could stretch beyond the next twelve months.

A well-positioned home—whether rented or owned—becomes a stabilizing foundation. It is where routines take root and planning becomes easier. Predictability replaces negotiation. We stop wondering what next year's rent increase will be. We stop reacting to someone else's timeline.

This was not just a financial decision. It was a decision about leverage and permanence. This is what margin has always been meant to support.

Housing choices often drift toward what looks impressive rather than what works.

Some homes are built to be seen. You walk into a towering foyer that feels more like a hotel lobby than a place to live. The ceiling stretches two stories high. A chandelier hangs where no one ever looks. Rooms sit unused, arranged more for impression than daily life. Everything signals success. Very little supports how you actually live.

Prestige increases expectations. Function reduces friction. The difference is subtle at first. But over time, it compounds.

We can rent when flexibility matters more than permanence. We buy when permanence matters more than flexibility.

We often make mistakes because we choose permanence too early. Rent when income is uncertain, job or school location may change, or savings are still accumulating. Buy when income is stable, job or school location is certain, and you will still have margin after purchase. The difference is not just financial. It is structural.

The Housing Decision is a Tradeoff

Renting	Buying
Flexible	Stable
Lower commitment	Higher commitment
No equity	Builds equity
Easier to adjust	Harder to adjust
Lower upfront cost	Higher upfront cost
Predictable short-term cost	Variable long-term cost
Mobility for opportunities	Anchored to location
Less responsibility	Full responsibility
Rent may rise over time	Fixed mortgage possible
No housing market exposure	Exposed to housing cycles
Optionality	Psychological ownership

This minimalist table shows the tradeoffs between renting and buying. Ownership builds equity, but it also introduces variability. Costs do not end with the purchase. Renting requires much less responsibility but provides no equity. Your costs are at the whim of outside parties.

Both ownership and renting can build wealth. Only one should fit your life right now.

Dual Returns: Equity and Stability

Housing produces two kinds of return. The first is financial. Equity builds through ownership over time. Each mortgage payment increases ownership. Over years, that ownership can become a meaningful net worth. For many families, a home becomes their first durable asset.

The second return is structural. Stability reduces background uncertainty. Planning horizons extend. Decisions become less reactive. That stability compounds. While the investment return from housing shows up on paper, stability shows up in your decisions.

Both matter, but they do not behave the same.

Renting can provide stability through flexibility and lower financial commitment. Ownership can provide stability through permanence and equity, but it also introduces variability. Costs do not end at the mortgage. They expand through maintenance, repairs, and time. Homeownership often includes ongoing maintenance costs (commonly estimated at 1–2% of home value annually, though actual costs vary).

Both renting and owning can support wealth when chosen intentionally.

The mistake is assuming one is always superior. The real question is whether your housing reduces pressure or amplifies it. When the decision fits your life, financial and emotional benefits reinforce each other. When it doesn't, leverage magnifies stress.

This chapter is not about buying a home. There is no universally right answer between renting and owning.

The right choice is the one that supports your life at this stage. It is about positioning housing to reduce pressure, not to create it. What grows most in stable housing is not only equity. It is clarity.

Here is a simple test for you: if your housing costs prevent you from saving consistently or building reserves, the structure is too tight even if you can technically afford it.

Housing and Cognitive Load

A stable home reduces the number of decisions you have to make, but only when the cost is manageable.

When payments stretch beyond people's comfort, the opposite effect takes place. Their attention narrows. Their decisions become reactive. They don't have much mental clarity. Pressure consumes their attention.

One of the least discussed benefits of stable housing is cognitive. Renters constantly have questions nervously running in the back of their mind. Will the rent increase? Will the lease be renewed? What if the landlord sells? What if we have to move again? Even financially secured renters feel that uncertainty.

But overextended homeowners experience another form of pressure. Large mortgages, rising costs, and inflexible commitments can create their own background stress.

When housing becomes stable—whether through renting or owning—something subtle happens. Your mind clears. You stop scanning listings every few months "just in case." You stop bracing for unexpected changes. The mental load decreases.

And when that load disappears, other forms of wealth begin to grow, such as focus, creativity, long-term thinking, and emotional calm.

Psychological freedom compounds the same way money does. You see it in behavior: longer horizons, fewer forced decisions, less reaction under pressure. A home is not only our shelter, but also our emotional architecture. The hidden return is mental clarity.

The Emotional Wealth of Stability

There is a common myth that every home is a great investment. It isn't.

A home becomes the wrong decision when flexibility matters more than permanence. If income is volatile, location uncertain, or leverage eliminates margin, ownership can amplify fragility.

In those seasons, renting is often the disciplined choice. Renting rarely builds housing equity, but it can protect margin and flexibility while life is still evolving. Ownership only becomes powerful when stability already exists.

The mistake is not renting or buying. The mistake is choosing housing that increases pressure.

But here is the deeper truth. A home does not need to be a perfect investment to pay off. Stability is the real yield. **Better housing decisions do not maximize returns. They minimize regret.** It improves the quality of every decision that follows. People make better decisions when they feel secure. They think more clearly. They take fewer reckless risks.

Housing becomes fragile when it removes your ability to adjust.

An overextended mortgage. Low liquidity after closing. Payments that depend on everything going right. At first, nothing feels wrong, but unexpected costs rarely arrive at convenient times. A broken water heater. A leaking roof. Repairs that can't be delayed. These are not rare events; they are a regular part of ownership.

Without margin, they turn inconvenience into pressure. Then conditions change.

What was manageable becomes tight. Decisions become reactive. The issue is not the home. It is the structure around it. When housing absorbs too much margin, it stops being a foundation. It becomes a constraint on every future decision.

A home should give you room to think, not force you to react.

Some of the signs that your housing is becoming fragile include:

- Costs leave little room to save
- Unexpected expenses create stress
- Decisions depend on income staying stable
- You feel locked in rather than supported

If two or more are true, the structure is fragile.

A stable home—even a modest one—creates a psychological foundation that spreadsheets cannot measure. It improves judgment. A stable environment supports routines, family life, and long-term planning. When your surroundings are predictable, the future becomes easier to protect.

That is the emotional wealth of housing. A home may not always produce extraordinary financial returns. But stability almost always produces better decisions. And better decisions compound. **Renting well is often wiser than buying poorly.**

Common Frictions

Barrier 1: "If I don't buy now, I'll miss out."

This is usually pressure, not analysis. **The pressure to buy is rarely financial. It is social.**

Personal finance responds to consequences, not urgency. Buying before income, savings, and margin are ready turns stability into stress.

Missing a purchase is recoverable; being locked into a fragile housing commitment is harder to unwind.

Barrier 2: "A bigger home means I'm succeeding in life."

This confuses status with support.

Homes are not scorecards; they are environments. When housing becomes a signal, fixed costs expand, and optionality shrinks.

Success isn't what your home says about you; it's what your home allows you to do next.

Barrier 3: "Stability will make me complacent."

This confuses calm with stagnation.

Stability doesn't cap ambition—it removes background noise. When housing pressure is low, you can take smarter risks elsewhere without putting everything at stake.

A solid foundation doesn't slow growth. It makes growth survivable.

Chapter 5 Summary

- Housing is neither just shelter nor just an investment. It is a structural decision that shapes behavior.
- The right housing position changes over time. Renting can provide flexibility early. Ownership can provide stability later.
- Stability is the real return. Predictable housing costs reduce pressure and improve quality of decisions.
- Housing works when it preserves margin. Stretching for prestige erodes flexibility.
- A well-positioned home supports compounding elsewhere by reducing volatility at the foundation.
- This pillar strengthens money by preserving margin and avoiding overcommitment, saves time by maintaining flexibility and optionality, and keeps energy by reducing cognitive load and ongoing financial pressure.

Chapter 5 Action Plan

1. **Assess your readiness, not the amount of pressure**

you can take. Rent when flexibility is valuable. Buy only when income, savings, and reserves comfortably support ownership.

2. **Set a housing ceiling.** Choose monthly costs that preserve margin rather than stretch lifestyle.
3. **Optimize for stability.** Favor predictability, function, and livability over prestige or speculation.
4. **Stress-test the payment.** Ask whether it can survive income disruption, repairs, or life changes.
5. **Protect liquidity.** Keep reserves after purchase. Ownership without a buffer is fragile.

Where you live shapes how you use your money, your time, and your energy. That is why housing is not an investment decision but a life decision.

The next pillar focuses on preparing for the future, building systems that absorb change without forcing reactive decisions.

Chapter 6

Prepare for the Future

Preparedness brings safety.

"The purpose of insurance is to protect you from a catastrophe you cannot afford."

— Dave Ramsey[13]

When Amy's phone rang, it wasn't a financial emergency in the traditional sense. There was no market crash, no job loss, no sudden bill demanding payment by midnight. It was quieter, and worse. Her child needed care—unexpected, ongoing, and non-negotiable. Time mattered. Presence mattered. The cost arrived either way.

What made the moment different wasn't luck. It was preparation built into her life.

Amy didn't scramble for credit. She didn't borrow from family. She didn't have to choose between attending to her child and protecting her finances. She used her emergency fund as it was intended. It did more than cover costs; it gave her time to focus on her child, and the energy to respond without panic. It served as a buffer between life's demands and panic.

That's what preparation looks like in real life. It's not perfect timing, but systems stepping in when something goes wrong.

It works across three resources. It allows money to provide the buffer, time to create room to respond, and energy to remain available for what matters most.

This chapter is about building protection—not out of fear, but out of responsibility. It's about recognizing that no institution, employer, or system cares about your future as much as you do.

Most people think of saving as a personal act—something you do for your future, your goals, your peace of mind.

Moments like this one reveal the truth: you don't save only for yourself, but for everyone who depends on you, directly or indirectly. Your children. Your partner. Your parents. The people who pay when you aren't ready.

Life doesn't give warnings before it tests you. Health changes. Jobs end. Family needs arise. Then money stops being abstract. It becomes protection.

At some point, you become the backup plan. Once you accept that, saving and insurance seem less pessimistic. They become infrastructure.

Beth Anne didn't know when her emergency fund would be needed. She only knew that if the moment ever came, she wanted to respond with clarity instead of chaos. It preserved her dignity in a moment that could have stripped it away.

The goal of preparation isn't to eliminate risk. It's to survive financially intact over time, and emotionally, to absorb shocks without panic, and to protect the people you love.

Because the real cost isn't in preparing for what might happen, it's in being unprepared when something inevitably does happen. When you're ready, you don't just feel safer. You move steadily.

Chapter 4 was about protecting capital. This chapter is about protecting continuity—your ability to keep living, deciding, and showing up when life disrupts your plans.

Saving Is Responsibility, Not Selfishness

For a long time, I thought saving was a selfish act. Money saved felt like money taken away—from family, from duties, from now. That illusion didn't survive responsibility.

Supporting my family back in China forever changed how I understood money. When I sent money home during tight months, it wasn't generosity, but a duty. Love in numbers. I knew that if I failed financially, it wouldn't just affect me.

I remember when I first started my career. Sending money home meant doing the math three times before I hit "transfer" making sure I could still cover my own expenses. My parents took on more financial risk than most. If something went wrong, it would affect me. Some nights, I worried everything we were holding together might snap. Still, I sent the money anyway. In those moments, saving turned from a personal habit into a shared duty.

Saving protects more than money. It preserves time when others need you, and energy when decisions matter most.

Parents age, children arrive, health changes, and jobs disappear without warning. When those moments hit, savings stop being abstract and become protection. Preparation becomes responsibility.

Saving is not just discipline. It is a responsibility over time—the decision that if something goes wrong, the people you love won't pay the price. That shift changes everything. Money stops being optimization and becomes stewardship under uncertainty. This step is about more than money. It's about dignity. It's about being someone others can lean on.

No One Else Is the Backup

Most people move through life assuming someone else has them covered: a stable employer, a generous benefits package, or a functioning system that will step in when things go wrong. Until it doesn't.

Jobs end. Health changes. Markets tighten. Benefits get cut. Even good companies make choices that don't protect you. The uncomfortable truth is this: no institution cares about your future as much as you do.

High income often creates the illusion of safety, but it also creates fragility. Fixed obligations rise, flexibility shrinks, and when income is interrupted, the fall is faster and harder than people expect. That's why many high earners feel exposed.

At some point, I stopped thinking of saving and insurance as optional. I began to see them as vital parts of my foundation. Not exciting, but essential. Like electricity, you only notice it when it's gone.

That shift led to a simple realization: I am my own safety net.

Being your own safety net doesn't mean expecting disaster; it means refusing to be surprised by it. Illness is not hypothetical; it will eventually happen one way or another, guaranteed. Slow months are not rare. Family emergencies don't schedule themselves around pay cycles. And relying on luck—or hoping nothing goes wrong—is not a strategy.

So you build buffers. You save regularly, not when it's convenient. You create an emergency fund before you feel ready. You use insurance to transfer risks that could cause irreversible damage.

Preparedness isn't pessimism. It's realism paired with optimism.

This is not about expecting the worst. It's about being ready enough that the worst doesn't define your decisions. It's believing life will continue and deciding you'll be ready when it does.

Preparation doesn't make you cautious; it creates optionality in how you use your time, and how you direct your energy under pressure. When downside is covered, you can play a longer game.

When you become your own safety net, something subtle changes. Fear loses its grip. You stop feeling one paycheck away from panic. You stop overreacting to temporary setbacks. You make decisions from a position of strength rather than urgency.

The future will arrive whether you prepare or not. Age. Health. Responsibility. They don't wait for confidence. One day, your future self will look back at the systems you built and feel gratitude—not for speed or cleverness, but for readiness.

The Hidden Cost of Being Unprepared

There is a cost to preparing for the future. Insurance premiums feel annoying. Emergency funds feel slow. Saving "just in case" can feel unnecessary when life is calm. The cost of not preparing is often greater, and it tends to arrive at the worst moment.

When people avoid preparation, it's rarely because they don't understand the logic. It's because preparation feels invisible. You pay for something and hope you never use it. You set money aside and pray nothing goes wrong. The benefit is quiet. The payoff is absence, and absence is hard to value.

I learned this lesson long before I could name it.

My father worked hard. He took risks to build businesses that could support our family. None of them failed overnight, but instead slowly, through thin margins, high debt, and the absence of a real buffer.

I still remember creditors coming to our home. Their voices were calm, but the message was heavy. I witnessed my mother borrowing money from acquaintances. She did it urgently and quietly to protect my father from legal issues.

No one explained it to me, but I understood enough: the damage wasn't just financial but emotional. It consumed time that could not be recovered, and energy that shaped every decision that followed.

People often do everything "right" on paper—budgeting carefully, investing consistently, avoiding debt. Then one event hits—a medical issue, job loss, or family crisis—and years of progress unravel. Because protection is missing.

The math is brutal. Without an emergency fund, small problems become big ones. The damage isn't just financial—it's emotional. Stress compounds faster than interest, and fear takes over the decision-making process.

Preparation doesn't guarantee comfort, but it does guarantee continuity in spendable money, time to respond, and clear decision-making under pressure. It gives you time, choices, and dignity when things go wrong. It creates a buffer. With a safety net, problems stay problems. Without one, they become disasters.

What most people miss is that preparation compounds, too. Each small buffer reduces stress. Reduced stress improves judgment. Better judgment prevents avoidable mistakes. Avoiding big mistakes preserves wealth.

The truth is both simple and uncomfortable: you can recover from most mistakes, but you cannot recover easily from a disaster you didn't prepare for.

The cost of preparation is predictable, but the cost of being unprepared is unlimited. Pay the smaller, predictable price—on your terms—before life charges you the larger one.

The Emotional Wealth of Safety

There is a kind of peace that isn't about optimism or confidence in your skills. It comes from knowing that if life goes wrong, you won't fall apart. That is the emotional wealth of safety.

When you have savings, insurance, and buffers in place, something shifts. Your nervous system relaxes. You sleep better. You don't panic at every unexpected bill or feel trapped by your next paycheck. You respond instead of bracing. You gain time to think and the energy to act with clarity.

Most people think financial security is just a number, but it's also the emotional absence of fear—the confidence that your family won't be exposed to bad luck or a temporary setback. This kind of safety doesn't make you reckless. It makes you brave. You can think in the long term, say no to bad opportunities, and take risks that are measured instead of desperate.

That's the paradox: preparation doesn't shrink your life, but expands it.

It protects your money, gives you time to respond, and preserves the energy to make better decisions. The emotional return arrives early. The moment you know you're covered, something inside you settles. You carry yourself differently. You trust your decisions more. That's real wealth—not the thrill of gains, but the confidence that no matter what happens, you have a floor beneath you.

Safety is not the absence of risk. It's the presence of resilience built in advance. And that resilience is what allows everything else in this system to work.

Common Frictions

Barrier 1: "Nothing bad has happened yet."

This is not evidence. It's timing.

Calm periods make preparation feel unnecessary because the benefit is invisible. But protection must exist *before* it's needed. Once disruption arrives, it's too late to build buffers without cost.

Preparation isn't a reaction. It's a decision made in advance.

Barrier 2: "Insurance feels like wasted money."

This is a misunderstanding of purpose.

Insurance isn't designed to produce returns. It exists to prevent irreversible damage. You're not paying for profit—you're paying to stay in the game when something goes wrong.

The value of insurance is measured by what it prevents, not what it earns.

Barrier 3: "Preparing for disasters feels pessimistic."

This confuses realism with fear.

Preparation doesn't assume things will go wrong. It acknowledges that some things eventually do. When protection is in place, optimism becomes safer, not naïve.

Preparedness doesn't shrink life. It steadies it.

Chapter 6 Summary

- Preparation is responsibility, not pessimism. You save for everyone who depends on you.
- You cannot rely on any institution for your backup plan. Stability comes from what you build yourself.

- The cost of not preparing is unlimited. One uncovered shock can undo years of progress.

- Safety changes behavior. When downside is covered, decisions improve.

- Emotional wealth comes from resilience—the confidence that shocks are survivable.

- This pillar strengthens money by building buffers and transferring catastrophic risk, expands time by creating space to respond without urgency, and maintains energy by reducing fear and enabling clear decision-making under stress.

Chapter 6 Action Plan

1. **Build a real emergency fund.** Maintain an emergency fund in spendable cash worth three to six months of essential expenses. Although it sounds boring, it's reliable.

2. **Close insurance gaps.** Make sure you have insurance covering your health, life, disability, home/apartment, and car, so you can transfer catastrophic risk to the insurance providers.

3. **Automate protection.** Set up the savings and insurance payments automatically without reminders.

4. **Stress-test your life.** Ask yourself, *"What fails if income stops for three months?"* Fix the weakest point.

5. **Write a safety plan for yourself.** It can be as little as

one sentence—for example, "*I don't carry risks that can ruin me.*"

When your foundation is secure and your life is prepared for disruption, effort becomes a choice rather than a necessity. You protect more than money; you protect your time to act deliberately, and the energy to pursue opportunity without pressure.

The next pillar is about strengthening your earning power, so income grows from clarity and leverage, not urgency or risk-taking under pressure.

CHAPTER 7

PROPEL YOUR EARNING POWER

GROW YOUR SKILLS WITH A PURPOSE.

"Your earning power is a muscle. The more you use it, the more it grows."
— Barbara Corcoran [14]

Barbara Corcoran didn't start as a mogul, an investor, or a television personality. She began as a waitress in New York City, earning about a thousand dollars a month and feeling stuck. With no prestigious degree, no powerful connections, and no obvious edge, she faced a hard truth: income wouldn't change unless she did.

So, she made a small but decisive move. She borrowed $1,000, quit her job, and started a small real estate company in New York City. There was nothing glamorous about it in the beginning. After numerous cold calls, awkward pitches, and constant rejections, Corcoran grasped a key insight: income rises when skills rise.

She built skills relentlessly, including sales, communication, negotiation, and reading people. Each improvement was modest in itself, but together they stacked. They didn't just increase her income; they gave her more control over her time, and allowed her to focus her energy on higher-value work. Over time, those skills evolved into leverage.

Many people who attempt similar moves fail. What made this outcome different wasn't courage; it was her decision to build skill before leverage. We build this skill before leverage so that any move we make is survivable.

This chapter is about earning power as protection—not bold moves.

Earning power strengthens more than our income. It allows our money to accumulate, our time to become more flexible, and our energy to be directed where it matters most.

That sounds obvious, but most people don't live that way. They wait for better timing, better markets, or better bosses, instead of becoming someone whom opportunities look for.

I once believed progress worked the same way, and that patience alone would eventually be rewarded. But careers don't change in leaps; they change in small but steady steps.

In my case, becoming a CFO wasn't a lucky break; it was a staircase. Each step up was earned through skill, consistency, and deliberate improvement. Neither the exams I passed, the responsibilities I took on, nor the trust I built quietly over time changed everything. But together, they did.

This chapter explains how that staircase is built, and why income rises when value compounds. The principles that follow apply whether you are in finance, technology, operations, medicine, management, or anything else. Titles and industries change; the mechanics of earning power do not.

Your income doesn't grow just because you're working harder. This is not about doing more. It's about becoming more valuable in ways that compound over time.

As this happens, you gain more control over how you spend your time and where you direct your energy. Your income grows because you become harder to replace. You compound your skills, reputation, and trust from other people. Over time, people pay more for certainty than for effort.

The Staircase to CFO, Not the Leap

People often look at income growth and imagine a leap, such as a lucky break, a single promotion, or some other moment when everything suddenly changes. That story is comforting but rarely true. In reality, earning power grows like a staircase, step by step.

The staircase isn't smooth. The steps are uneven. Some lead nowhere, while others require moving sideways—or briefly backward—before you can climb again. Progress rarely feels orderly when you're going through it; it only looks linear in hindsight.

My own income didn't grow because the world decided to reward me. It grew because I kept becoming more useful.

Early in my career, there was nothing glamorous about my work. Long hours. Weekends were spent preparing for exams instead of relaxing. It didn't feel like it was paying off. There were no instant rewards. No dramatic jumps. Just steady effort applied in the same direction. That's how the staircase works.

Passing exams, earning trust, and taking on responsibility weren't lucky breaks—they were steps in the same direction. Each step helped me develop skills that accumulated over time. I gained technical knowledge, judgment, communication, reliability, and trust. Every credential earned expanded what I could handle. Every responsibility handled well increased trust.

Income follows value, and value compounds when you keep adding to it. That compounding shows up in more than money; it increases how much control you have over your time, and reduces the energy required to prove yourself repeatedly.

The risk is assuming that value automatically increases with effort. It doesn't. Value compounds when effort is directed and always adjusted to changing circumstances. Otherwise, you are simply accumulating activity. Earning power grows through reliability as much as talent. Those traits reshape your trajectory.

The staircase also explains why comparison is dangerous. Someone might seem "ahead" of you today, but that is because you didn't see their earlier steps.

Optimizing your earning power is not about chasing shortcuts. It's about steady improvement until results appear. You learn one skill, complete one project, pass one exam, and reinforce your reputation. The jump in your earning power doesn't require a leap, just steady steps in the same direction.

The Most Profitable Investment Is You

Warren Buffett once said, "The best investment you can make is in yourself." It seems simple, even obvious, but many people don't realize how true that is.

Skill compounds more reliably than capital, because it improves how you earn money, how you use your time, and how effectively you apply your energy.

Markets fluctuate. Roles change. Firms restructure. But skills carry forward. When you improve them, the payoff shows up everywhere at once: higher income, better roles, and more control over your time.

The mechanism is straightforward. Small improvements, applied consistently, accumulate. This approach feels slow because it avoids volatility, but slow, controlled growth makes earning power durable. A modest weekly gain doesn't feel meaningful in isolation, but over time it becomes decisive.

The advantage is repetition without interruption. This is why self-investment works when so many other strategies fail. The target is small enough to sustain, and easy enough to repeat. **You need rhythm—learning one new concept, practicing one uncomfortable skill, or refining one process.** Each action is unremarkable on its own, but together they change how valuable you are.

As skills compound, something else grows alongside income: optionality. You gain more control over your time, and channel your energy toward higher-impact work instead of constant effort. You qualify for bigger challenges. You're trusted with larger decisions. You're harder to replace. People pay you more because your judgment improves.

That's the durable advantage of investing in yourself. There's no market volatility, no external competition for access, and no ceiling imposed by financial cycles. The returns are durable. Money compounds when left alone; skill compounds when practiced—and, unlike money, it survives role changes, market cycles, and organizational shifts.

Luck Is Built, Not Found

People love to explain success with the word "luck." It makes failure feel excusable, and it removes responsibility. But after watching careers compound—my own included—I've learned something different: what most people call luck in this situation is just the moment someone's preparation becomes visible.

Opportunities rarely arrive without context. They show up when someone has already built the skills, credibility, and capacity to handle them. From the outside, it looks sudden, but from the inside, it's earned. The pattern is consistent:

- Skills are built first.
- Trust is earned.
- Margin funds experiment.
- Time allows those experiments to play out.
- Energy sustains the effort required to reach them.
- Optionality emerges over time.

I've seen this repeatedly, including in my own career. Roles didn't open because I chased them; they opened because the groundwork had already been laid, including exams passed, responsibilities handled well, and reputation earned over the years. When timing aligned, there was no scramble. There was readiness.

This is why "getting lucky" is rarely about bold moves. It's about sequencing. You don't abandon earning power to chase upside; you strengthen earning power, so that upside is inevitable. Luck favors consistent performers with reputations for reliability, who remain all-in even when progress feels invisible.

You can't manufacture luck on demand, but you can increase its surface area. Every skill you sharpen expands the problems you can solve. Every promise you keep compounds trust. Every layer enables the next. The paradox is simple: the less you chase luck, the more often it seems to find you. Luck rewards positioning.

You don't chase opportunity by taking risks. You qualify for it by becoming harder to replace.

The Emotional Wealth of Mastery

As earning power grows, the primary benefit is not income. It is durability.

When skills are deep and portable, you are no longer dependent on any single employer, title, or market cycle. What you carry forward is not a role, but capability—judgment, competence, and the ability to solve problems under pressure. That portability changes how uncertainty feels. You are no longer trading time for security, and your energy is no longer consumed by proving your value.

Setbacks become survivable. Transitions feel less threatening. Decisions slow down. This is the emotional wealth of mastery. It's not bravado, not arrogance, but calm confidence built on capability.

Earlier in my career, money felt like a fragile buffer. If income dipped or conditions changed, pressure rose immediately. Progress felt conditional—dependent on approval, timing, or external stability. As my skills grew, that fragility eased. Not because risk disappeared, but because exposure changed.

I noticed the shift before I saw it in the numbers. I negotiated differently. I stopped reacting to short-term noise. I felt less urgency to prove myself in every situation. Options appeared not because I chased them, but because I had become capable of handling them.

Mastery reshapes behavior. When you trust your ability to recover, you take fewer defensive risks. You walk away from situations that don't compound. You choose roles, projects, and environments more deliberately. You stop mistaking motion for progress. This is not confidence rooted in outcomes. It is confidence rooted in preparation.

Money can buffer volatility, but mastery reduces dependence on it. Income protects today; capability protects tomorrow. It increases what you can earn, how you use your time, and how effectively you direct your energy. Over time, this creates a reinforcing loop.

Portable skills reduce fear. Reduced fear improves judgment. Better judgment leads to better decisions. Better decisions compound both income and opportunity. That loop—not income alone—is what creates long-term agency.

When earning power is built deliberately, your future stops feeling fragile. It starts to feel resilient. And resilience is what allows everything else in this system to work.

Common Frictions

Barrier 1: "It's risky to change direction."

This is true but incomplete.

Staying still carries risk, too. Skills decay. Relevance fades. Optionality shrinks silently. The risk of change is visible; the risk of standing still compounds in the background.

Earning power grows when motion is intentional, not impulsive.

Barrier 2: "Focusing on money feels shallow."

This confuses motives with outcomes.

Earning power isn't about greed. It's about leverage—the ability to support others, absorb shocks, and choose more freely. Money is not the goal; it's the amplifier.

Growing earning power increases responsibility, not emptiness.

Barrier 3: "I don't have time."

This is usually a bandwidth problem, not a time problem.

When life is full, growth must be designed, not squeezed in. Small, repeatable investments in skills compound faster than sporadic bursts of effort.

Earning power grows through systems, not intensity.

Chapter 7 Summary

- Earning power compounds like capital. Income is a lagging indicator of skill and judgment.

- Careers grow by stair steps, not leaps. Small improvements accumulate gradually over time.
- Luck is built through preparation. Opportunities favor those already positioned.
- Skills create optionality. Mastery reduces dependence on any single role or employer.
- Emotional wealth comes from capability. Calm grows when value is portable.
- Increasing your skills strengthens money by increasing income and long-term earning capacity; expands time by creating flexibility and expanding optionality; and maintains energy by focusing effort on higher-value work and improving decision quality.

Chapter 7 Action Plan

1. **Choose one compounding skill.** Choose a skill that raises your ceiling: communication, analysis, leadership, sales. One focus beats five hobbies.
2. **Schedule a weekly mastery block.** Set up a time block on the same day of the week, same time. Forty-five minutes is enough if it happens every week.
3. **Make reliability visible.** You deliver on time, close loops, and document work. Trust is your multiplier.
4. **Buy one lever per quarter.** Enroll in a course, book a

mentor call, purchase a tool, or obtain a credential. One intentional upgrade every 90 days.

5. **Track reps, not praise**. Log the number of hours you practiced, projects shipped, and problems solved. Raises lag; reps predict them.

Earning power raises the ceiling. It increases your income, gives you more control over your time, and allows you to direct your energy where it matters most.

Next, you'll see how these seven pillars work as a system, so progress stops depending on willpower.

VIRTUOUS CYCLE OF THE 7 PILLARS OF WEALTH

"The structure of a system determines its behavior."
— Donella H. Meadows, *Thinking in Systems: A Primer* [15]

By now, you've seen each of the seven pillars individually. Each one strengthens a different part of your financial life: margin, stability, protection, preparation, and earning power. But the real power of the framework doesn't come from any single pillar. It comes from how they reinforce one another.

Together, the pillars form a self-reinforcing system. This system operates across three resources: money flows through it, time compounds within it, and energy determines how smoothly it runs. Each step reduces friction for the next, including financial friction, time pressure, and the energy required to keep the system running.

Margin makes saving easier. Savings make protection possible. Protection creates stability. Stability allows preparation. Preparation builds confidence. Confidence supports stronger earning power. And higher earning power creates greater margin, thus starting the system again.

Over time, the system begins to carry more of the load. Money requires less manual control. Time begins to work in your favor. Energy is no longer consumed by constant decision-making. Progress feels less forced. Decisions become calmer. Small actions begin to compound. Each pillar strengthens the next. As the cycle repeats, stability increases, fragility declines, and wealth compounds.

The 7 Pillars Wealth Flywheel

Self-Reinforcing Wealth-Building Cycle

The order of the sequence in the above illustration matters, because each pillar creates the conditions that allow the next pillar to work. Each strengthens a different constraint, whether that's money, time, or energy.

The flywheel begins with margin. Paying yourself first creates space. That space allows spending to become intentional, which leads to consistent savings. Savings create momentum, and protection ensures setbacks do not erase progress. Stability in housing and preparation for the future reduce volatility in life's largest risks. Finally, stronger earning power expands the system's capacity, making the next cycle easier.

How the Sequence Creates Leverage

Here is the cycle at work.

1. Pay Yourself First → Create Margin

Paying yourself first creates margin. Without margin, decisions are reactive.

Margin does not feel like progress at first. It feels restrictive. However, it changes the environment immediately. With margin in place, money stops being a constant negotiation. You stop operating at the edge. That space makes the next pillar possible.

But that space is fragile. One expense, one lifestyle upgrade, or one month of inattention can erase it. That's why margin does more than protect money. It gives you time to think and energy to make better decisions.

2. Prioritize Your Spending → Sustain Margin

Once margin exists, the risk is leakage. Prioritizing spending stops it. This pillar turns restraint into structure. You decide in advance what deserves resources. The result is that margin holds.

Without this pillar, margin decays silently. Income rises. Flexibility does not.

3. Power Your Savings → Build Momentum

At this stage, progress becomes visible. Accounts grow. Buffers form. Time begins to work for you. The numbers may feel small, but the direction is clear.

Momentum matters psychologically. It reduces second-guessing. With momentum, protection becomes relevant instead of theoretical; without momentum, discipline becomes brittle.

Time begins to work for you, reducing the need for constant effort and preserving energy.

4. Protect Your Savings → Guard Progress

Protection preserves momentum by limiting downside.

Protection does not prevent setbacks. It limits how far setbacks can push you backward, and how much rebuilding they require. It changes behavior more than your account balances. When the downside is bounded, judgment improves. Without protection, every market drawdown forces a decision. Those decisions compound against you.

Protection preserves not just capital but time by preventing large setbacks, and energy by reducing reactive decisions.

5. Position Your Housing Wisely → Establish Grounding

Housing is not about maximizing return. It is about stability. Positioned wisely—whether rented or owned—housing reduces uncertainty in one of life's largest recurring expenses, so short-term shocks don't force long-term financial decisions.

When your living situation is stable, long-term thinking becomes easier and reactive decisions decline; when housing is unstable, long-term thinking collapses into short-term survival, even at high income levels.

Stability here amplifies every prior pillar. It stabilizes how you use your time and reduces the energy spent managing uncertainty.

6. Prepare for the Future → Create Safety

Preparation formalizes resilience. This pillar changes identity. You stop relying on luck and start operating with a floor. Fear loses leverage. Without safety, disruptions become turning points. When safety is present, optionality emerges. Safety creates time to respond and preserves energy under stress.

7. Propel Your Earning Power → Expand Capacity

Earning power expands the system's ceiling.

Skills compound differently than assets. They expand options, improve judgment, and reduce replacement risk. Higher earning power does not merely raise income. It increases the system's tolerance for error and experimentation.

With capacity expanded, margin becomes easier to rebuild, savings accelerate, and protection strengthens. It expands not just income over time, but also control and the ability to direct energy toward higher-value work. The cycle turns again with less resistance.

Why Progress Becomes Easier Over Time

One full turn looks like this:

You pay yourself first and create margin. Margin turns spending from reactive to deliberate. Deliberate spending becomes consistent saving. Saving justifies protection, which prevents routine shocks from becoming reversals.

With downside contained, housing decisions stay conservative. Stable housing lowers volatility in monthly obligations. Lower volatility makes preparation easier. Preparation creates safety. Safety frees attention. Freed attention expands earning power, making the next round of margin easier to rebuild.

The outcome is not about speed. It is repeatable progress. Money compounds. Time becomes more available. Energy is no longer drained by constant adjustment.

Early turns of the cycle feel slow because friction remains high. Habits are new. Buffers are thin. Resistance is loud. Later turns feel easier not because discipline improves, but because constraints have shifted. The cycle isn't smooth; income sometimes drops, habits slip, buffers thin, and confidence wobbles. The advantage is that you recover faster.

When one pillar weakens, the others shorten the distance back to stability. They restore money faster, preserve time, and prevent energy from being consumed by stress. The system absorbs more effort for you. Decisions require less willpower. Recovery from setbacks is faster.

This is why the pillars must be built in sequence and revisited. Skipping one weakens the loop. Overloading one creates an imbalance. **The ideal outcome is durability.**

What the System Changes

Over time, the pillars change how money, time, and energy feel. Time feels less compressed. Energy feels less strained. Stress gives way to predictability. Urgency gives way to judgment. Reaction gives way to intention.

This is not confidence in markets; it is confidence in structure. You are less dependent on timing or luck and more able to operate within a system designed to compound under pressure.

The system weakens when a pillar is skipped or overloaded. Growth without protection, or saving without capacity, creates imbalance. Systems fail from asymmetry. That is the virtuous cycle: a loop reinforced through use. It does not prevent mistakes. It helps you recover faster.

How to Use the System

The seven pillars are not meant to be executed once and set aside. They are meant to be used repeatedly.

Using the system begins with diagnosis, not labor. For example, if saving feels difficult, the issue may not be discipline; it may be that margin is too thin or spending is misaligned. Fixing the earlier pillar often removes the friction entirely.

When money feels heavy again, the problem is rarely discipline; more often it's due to imbalance. One pillar is carrying too much load, or another has been neglected long enough so that the system is under strain due to lopsided compensation.

In those moments, the most useful question is not "*What should I do next?*" Instead, it is "*Which part of the system is under pressure, and why*?"

Sometimes the issue is the sequence. For example, maybe earning power was expanded before margin and protection were strong enough to absorb it. Or perhaps growth continued while preparation lagged. Or spending crept upward while savings momentum slowed.

These are not failures; they are signals. Systems don't break loudly at first. They tighten. They require more effort to produce the same results. That friction provides useful information.

The goal is not about speed. It is stability under pressure.

Life will interrupt progress. Income drops, expenses spike, habits slip, and confidence wavers. The system works not because these disruptions disappear, but because their impact is contained.

When one pillar weakens, the others shorten the distance back to stability. You don't start over; you recalibrate. This is why perfection is unnecessary. What matters is alignment. As long as the pillars are aligned, small missteps remain survivable. When they drift out of sequence, even good decisions begin to feel unstable.

Over time, the system should be revisited as conditions change. New responsibilities arise. Families grow. Careers evolve. What once created stability may later create constraints. Using the system means noticing when that shift happens, and adjusting deliberately rather than reactively.

The system is not there to tell you what to do. It helps you manage money deliberately, use time effectively, and preserve energy under pressure. It changes the environment in which decisions are made. When the environment is stable, judgment improves. When judgment improves, effort compounds more reliably.

That is how the system is meant to be used—not as a checklist to complete and be done with, but as a structure to return to steadily and repeatedly whenever pressure shows up.

Summary

- The Seven Pillars of Wealth is a system, not a checklist. Progress comes from interaction, not completion.
- The right sequence creates leverage. The wrong order creates brittleness.
- Early results feel small because the system has not started carrying the load.
- Later progress feels easier because constraints shift and recovery becomes faster.
- Use the system by diagnosing imbalance and restoring alignment, not by forcing effort.
- This system strengthens money by aligning growth, protection, and stability; expands time by creating space, reducing setbacks, and enabling long-term thinking; and preserves energy by reducing friction, stress, and reactive decision-making.

Action Plan

1. **Diagnose pressure.** Ask which pillar is under strain right now.

2. **Restore sequence.** Rebuild margin and protection before chasing growth.

3. **Fix leakage.** Identify the biggest place money is escaping.

4. **Add one stabilizer.** Increase buffer, tighten insurance, or reduce a fixed cost.

5. **Rerun the loop weekly.** One small adjustment keeps the system aligned.

When money, time, and energy align, effort compounds instead of carrying the load.

Conclusion

When the Noise Softens

"Wealth consists not in having great possessions, but in having few wants."

— Epictetus[16]

When you first opened this book, money likely felt loud; not because you were careless or incapable, but because money never stopped demanding something from you. Bills, decisions, trade-offs, worries; they always press you, but never seem to rest.

Pause for a moment and notice what's different.

The noise has softened, and not just financially. You have more control over your time, and more energy for what matters. You are not the same person who started this book.

You now know how to keep the first slice, spend with intention instead of guilt, let time work instead of forcing outcomes, protect what you build, choose stability over pressure, prepare instead of hoping, and invest in yourself consistently.

This is not just a change in the numbers. It's an identity shift.

Most people who struggle with money don't do so because they lack discipline or intelligence. They struggle because money presses on them without structure, making every decision feel urgent, every surprise dangerous, and every setback personal.

What you've now built instead is a system, a structure designed to absorb pressure by reshaping the environment in which decisions are made.

Margin reduces urgency. Intentional spending preserves it. Savings create momentum. Protection limits reversals. Stable housing lowers volatility. Preparation creates safety. Earning power expands capacity.

The result isn't perfection but recoverability. Mistakes still happen and life still interrupts, but setbacks shrink, panic loses its power, and judgment returns faster.

That's what systems do. They don't remove risk; they contain it.

Over time, stress gives way to predictability, urgency to judgment, and reaction to intention. You no longer rely on confidence or motivation; you operate within a system designed to compound your money, time, and energy under pressure.

If doubts still whisper, that is normal. They often do when you step into something durable. Here is the truth you have earned: you do not need certainty or confidence every day. You have margin, structure, and resilience. That is more powerful than motivation.

So leave with this simple and sufficient action plan:

- Start small.

- Stay consistent.
- Protect your downside.
- Let time work.

Just steady behavior, repeated long enough to compound.

Now imagine your future, not as a fantasy but as a consequence. You no longer flinch at surprises. You decide calmly because options exist. Your money supports your life instead of dominating it.

Years from now, you won't remember the bank account balances. Instead, you will remember the feeling: confidence and control.

Money no longer presses because each dollar already has a role. Systems only work when they move. Movement always begins with a small, deliberate action.

So here is your first clear step. Within the next 24 hours, take one action that proves intention. Automate a transfer. Review one account. Write one rule. One move is enough to keep the system turning.

At the beginning of this book, we said that people don't feel broke because they lack money. They feel broke because money never stops pressing.

Now you understand why. Because there was no structure. Now there is. Pressure meets foundation. Effort meets direction. Motion meets momentum. You didn't escape reality. You built something solid inside it.

Close this book knowing this: **you are no longer chasing wealth; you are becoming someone around whom wealth grows.**

Apply the Seven Pillars

Turning Principles into Daily Decisions

The seven pillars are not meant to be used once and forgotten. They work as a system. When one pillar strengthens, it supports the others. Over time, the cycle begins to carry more of the load.

The 7 Pillars Wealth Flywheel

Self-Reinforcing Wealth-Building Cycle

The diagram above shows how the pillars reinforce one another. As the cycle repeats, stability increases, fragility declines, and wealth compounds.

Applying the pillars doesn't require perfection. It begins with small, deliberate actions. What matters most is direction and consistency.

Start with these steps:

1. *Pay yourself first — create margin before spending.*

2. *Prioritize your spending — direct money toward what matters, and sustain margin.*

3. *Power your savings — build steady momentum over time.*

4. *Protect your savings — guard progress from avoidable setbacks.*

5. *Position your housing wisely — anchor your finances with stability.*

6. *Prepare for the future — create safety before uncertainty arrives.*

7. *Propel your earning power — expand the system's long-term capacity.*

Readers who would like worksheets and tools to help implement the ideas in this book can access companion resources online:

https://xufenghua.com/wealth

These materials include practical exercises to help you apply the Seven Pillars framework to your financial and emotional life and build long-term wealth.

Further Resources & Influences

This book reflects ideas shaped over years of reading, listening, and practice. While the framework presented here is my own, many of the underlying principles—and my broader thinking on money, life, and decision-making—have been influenced by the work of thoughtful writers and practitioners.

Selected books:

1. *The Psychology of Money* — Morgan Housel
2. *The Most Important Thing* — Howard Marks
3. *The Richest Man in Babylon* — George S. Clason
4. *Atomic Habits* — James Clear
5. *Afford Anything* — Paula Pant
6. *Fooled by Randomness* — Nassim Nicholas Taleb

Selected podcasts and conversations:

Long-form conversations on decision-making, investing, and behavior under uncertainty, including:

1. *The Tim Ferriss Show* by Tim Ferriss

2. *Marriage, Kids and Money* by Andy Hill

3. *All the Hacks* by Chris Hutchins

For a more complete and updated list of books and resources that have influenced this framework and my broader thinking on money, life, and decision-making, please visit:

https://xufenghua.com/wealth

Notes

1. Howard Marks focuses on risk and market cycles, emphasizing that long-term success depends more on managing downside than chasing returns.

2. Morgan Housel focuses on the psychology of money, emphasizing how behavior, patience, and emotional control matter more than intelligence or optimization in long-term outcomes.

3. Boyette, Chris. "A Man Lived Quietly in a Mobile Home and Left $3.8 Million to His Town," CNN, June 29, 2023. https://www.cnn.com/2023/11/21/us/hinsdale-new-hampshire-town-donation

4. Paula Pant focuses on decision-making and trade-offs, emphasizing that money choices are about aligning resources with priorities rather than trying to optimize everything at once.

5. Haas, Lauryn. "I Have $25,000 in Credit Card Debt and a Six-Figure Job. I Fell Victim to Lifestyle Creep, and Inflation Didn't Help." *Business Insider*, 3 Sept. 2025, https://www.businessinsider.com/make-6-figures-27-have-25000-debt-lifestyle-creep-2025-9

6. Charlie Munger emphasized clear thinking, sound incentives, and avoiding obvious mistakes, believing that long-term success comes from judgment and patience rather than cleverness.

7. Anne Scheiber. *Wikipedia*, Wikimedia Foundation, last edited 2025, accessed on 4 Jan. 2026, https://en.wikipedia.org/wiki/Anne_Scheiber

8. Nassim Nicholas Taleb focuses on fragility, uncertainty, and the risk of ruin, arguing that long-term success depends on avoiding irreversible losses rather than maximizing upside.

9. https://www.federalreservehistory.org/essays/ltcm-near-fail ure

10. https://www.federalreservehistory.org/essays/ltcm-near-fail-ure

11. U.S. Securities and Exchange Commission. *SEC Charges Eight Social Media Influencers in $100 Million Stock Manipulation Scheme Promoted on Twitter and Discord.* 21 Dec. 2022, www.sec.gov/news/press-release/2022-221

12. Warren Buffett emphasizes patience, discipline, and risk management, often noting that a home's greatest value lies in stability and utility rather than its ability to generate outsized financial returns.

13. Dave Ramsey emphasizes behavioral discipline and basic safeguards, stressing that insurance exists not to optimize outcomes but to protect families from financial catastrophe when life goes wrong.

14. Barbara Corcoran emphasizes sales, confidence, negotiation, and resilience, often framing earning power as a muscle—the more you use it, test it, and stretch it, the stronger it becomes over time. She has discussed hiring and judgment extensively in interviews and on *Shark Tank*, emphasizing track record and reliability over credentials.

15. Donella H. Meadows studied how systems behave over time, emphasizing that outcomes are driven by structure and feedback loops, not by effort or intention alone.

16. Epictetus taught that peace and stability come from focusing on what you can control and letting go of what you cannot, especially in the face of uncertainty.

Acknowledgements

This book reflects ideas shaped over fifteen years of reading, listening, and practice. I'm grateful to the authors, podcast hosts, guests, and to the colleagues, mentors, and friends whose perspectives have deepened my understanding of wealth, behavior, and long-term thinking.

I would like to thank Dr. Wendy Jeffus for her encouragement and feedback on early drafts of this book. I am also grateful to Curtis Bramley and Dr. Vikrant Yadav for their thoughtful input. Curtis, in particular, helped validate the structure of the Seven Pillars and offered valuable editorial perspectives.

I'm grateful to Jason Pettus for his thoughtful editing and for helping to refine the manuscript's clarity and flow.

Finally, my deepest gratitude goes to my family for their patience, understanding, and steady support throughout the writing of this book.

About the Author

Xufeng (Bill) Hua is a hedge fund CFO with over 15 years of experience in investing, risk management, and financial strategy. He is a CFA charterholder and works at an institutional investment firm where decisions are evaluated not only by returns but also by durability.

He writes about wealth as a system that connects money, time, and energy, focusing on how people make decisions under pressure and how structure supports long-term progress. Bill grew up in rural China and built his career through education, discipline, and long-term thinking. His perspective is shaped as much by lived experience as by professional training.

Learn more at xufenghua.com, where you can subscribe to Compound Emotion, his weekly newsletter on building wealth across money, time, and energy.

Made in the USA
Coppell, TX
05 November 2026

11314455R00073